FORBUSH MEMORIAL LIBRARY
DISCARD
118 MAIN ST
WESTMINSTER MA 01473

MAY 2018

D1559584

Social Security Offset Penalties

WEP ~ GPO ~ Dual Entitlement

**School Teachers   Professors   Librarians
Police & Fire Dept.   City & State Employees
Bus Drivers   Janitors   School Lunch Workers**

*In 28 states, if you split your career between a
civil service position and a SS covered job you will
lose from 50% to 100% of your SS benefits.*

Jeanette A. Wicks

DISCARD

Copyright © Oct. 13, 2017 by Jeanette A. Wicks
Cover and interior by: Cactus Valley LLC

Published by: Cactus Valley LLC,
Grand Junction, CO 81501
Email: **cactusvalleyllc@yahoo.com**

No part of this publication may be reproduced, stored in a
retrieval system or transmitted in any form or by any means,
electronic, mechanical, photocopying, recording, scanning
or otherwise, except as permitted under Sections 107 or 108
of the 1976 United States Copyright Act, without the prior
written permission of the Publisher.

Requests to the Publisher for permissions:
Email: **cactusvalleyllc@yahoo.com**
Volume discounts are available

Limit of Liability/disclaimer of warranty: The publisher and
the author make no representations or warranties with respect
to the accuracy or completeness of the contents of this book
and specifically the advice and strategies contained herein may
not be suitable for every situation.

Readers should be aware that internet websites listed in this
book may have changed or disappeared between when the
book was written and when it is read.

ISBN 978-0-9986986-4-9 (paperback)
ISBN 978-0-9986986-5-6 (e-book)
ISBN 978-0-9986986-0-1 (e-pub)

10 9 8 7 6 5 4 3 2 1

Table of Contents

Chapter 1 – Overview...................... 1

A Word to the Wise............................... 2

In this book you will learn........................ 3

The WEP, GPO, and DE Regulations............. 4

States with Offset Penalties....................... 4

The 28 States with Private Pension Systems....... 6

Windfall Elimination Provision – WEP........... 7

Government Pension Offset – GPO............... 8

Dual Entitlement Offset – DE...................... 9

Program Operations Manual System POMS..... 10

The Social Security Act of 1935.................. 11

President Reagan.................................. 14

Commissioner of SS – Job Description............ 15

Chapter 2 – Private State Pensions..... 17

Employees Facing Offsets........................... 17

The Private Pension................................ 18

Beneficiaries – Be Careful........................ 19

FICA Taxes.. 19

Social Security Eligibility.......................... 21

No Refunds.. 21

Social Security Options............................ 22

    Book: *"Get What's Yours"*................... 22

Average SS Benefits.............................. 22

State Contact Information......................... 24

Table of Contents

Chapter 3 – Saving Social Security.... 25

The 1983-Refinancing Act 25
Social Security is Not Going Bankrupt.......... 26
Your Benefit Statements........................... 27
Substantial Earnings................................. 27
Who Gets Hurt?....................................... 30
The Offset Gauntlet.................................. 30
The SSA Guarantee.................................. 31
How Propaganda Fuels the Jealousy............. 32

Chapter 4 – Notification 35

Confused SS Staff & Confused Retirees......... 35
The Offset Fights..................................... 37
Kevin Brady and Richard Neal H.R.711......... 38
Three Big Mistakes.................................. 40
Need to Know Basis.................................. 41
SS Fantasy – A Reality Check..................... 42
The Elephant in the Room.......................... 43

Chapter 5 – Windfall Elimination Provision... 47

The Windfall Logic.................................. 48
Public Pension Payment Options............,..... 50
Specific Time Period................................. 51
POMS 00605.364..................................... 52
The Question is:WHY?............................... 53
Your "Modified" Lifetime Table.................. 56
Your "Real" Life Expectancy Table............... 56

Table of Contents

Your "True" Life Expectancy……….…..…...... 57

Offsets Forever……………………………...... 59

The SSA is Double Dipping……………...…... 60

The SS Trust Fund………………………….... 61

The "Matching" Funds Trick…………………... 63

The Privileged Few………………………….... 65

Equalization is Not Working…………………... 66

Congress……………………………………… 68

Book: *Get What's Yours*...……………………... 69

Chapter 6 – Government Pension Offset   71

Who is "NOT Dependent?"………...……..…... 72

What is earned income?.............................…….. 72

Who is Dependent…………………………….... 73

The Working Class vs The Idle Rich…………... 73

What's "W'ong" With This Picture…………….... 74

The Government Pension Offset states:………... 75

The Losers Club……………………………….... 76

Life Expectancy Confusion…………………….. 78

The Four SS LE Variations:……………………. 78

Floundering In The Dark……………………….. 81

Judge Olson…………………………………….. 83

No Adjustments……………………………….... 84

Chapter 7 – Dual Entitlement Rule…   87

Dual Entitlement……………………………….. 88

Example of How Your DE is Applied………….. 88

Table of Contents

Before 1983.. 91

Work is for Idiots................................ 93

Expenses... 94

The Great Migration............................ 96

Social Security – No Guarantees.............. 98

Annuities – A "Time Certain" Guarantee........ 100

Other Retirement Plans vs Social Security....... 101

Private Investment Account – Advantages....... 102

Your Social Security Account – Disadvantages.. 101

The Wealthy....................................... 103

Al Gore and The "Motherhood" Penalty.......... 104

Social Security.................................... 105

The Big Messy Offset Maze...................... 107

Retirement Benefits for Congress................. 108

Chapter 8 – The SS Trust Fund........ 109

The Civil War Pensions.......................... 109

Independent Regulatory Agency vs
          Independent Agency.................... 110

Executive Order by Bill Clinton 1993.............. 111

Former President Reagan......................... 112

Under The Gun.................................... 112

SSA Today.. 113

If The Money Runs Out 113

State Pension vs Social Security.................. 114

SS's Broken Promise.............................. 115

The Trustees Annual Report...................... 117

Your ½% Rate of Return.......................... 118

All The Eggs in One Basket....................... 120

Table of Contents

Outdated Investment Policies……..………... 122

The End of File and Suspend………..…….….. 123

Out of Touch………………….……...………... 124

Protecting Social Security…………......……... 125

Warren Buffet – Bonds are Terrible………….. 126

Chapter 9 – Above The Law ……….. 127

Fiduciary…………………….…………... 128

A Fool and His Money……………..………... 129

Entitlement it is NOT – It is Insurance...……... 129

SSA Fights Retirees……..………………….…….. 130

Absolute Power Corrupts Absolutely………….. 131

A Stacked Deck…………………………….... 131

Pirates Plunder…………………………….... 132

The Five Companies……………………..……... 133

The $104 Billion Afghanistan Bill…………….. 134

The $43 Million Gas Station……………..…….. 135

"Free Stuff" For The Rich………………….…….. 135

Cost to Eliminate the GPO / WEP……..……... 136

Nothing Contributed – Nothing Lost…………. 137

Who Really Loses?...................................……... 137

President Trump……………………………….. 137

Above The Law…………………………….….. 138

President Obama 2016……………….………... 139

Overview of the Antitrust Laws………...……... 140

The Sherman Act………………..……. 141

The Federal Trade Commission Act... 141

Bureau of Consumer Protection…….. 142

The Clayton Act…………………….. 142

V

Table of Contents

Single Firm Conduct............................ 143

Horizontal Conduct........................... 143

Breach of Contract............................. 144

Bad Faith.. 144

U.S. Supreme Court............................... 144

The McCarran-Ferguson Act...................... 145

Chapter 10 – Challenging The SSA.... 147

Boiling A Frog...................................... 148

It Takes Just One.................................. 149

The Rosa Parks Story............................ 150

Where To Begin................................... 150

    Write emails.................................... 150

    State what needs to change.................. 151

    What action do you want..................... 151

How To Eat an Elephant......................... 151

Contacting Your Representatives............... 152

Snail Mail & Social Media....................... 152

Your Local Library............................... 153

TV, Radio and Newspapers....................... 154

Groups, Unions & Organizations................ 155

Petitions... 155

Kevin Brady and Richard Neal.................. 156

What Happened Next?............................ 157

Teacher Shortages................................ 158

Boycotts.. 158

Who's on Your Side Dem vs Rep.................. 159

Table of Contents

Robert Reich Said……………………….….. 160

The Costly Migration……………………..... 161

Chasing Shadows……………………….….. 162

Chapter 11 – Issues To Appeal…….…... 163

The Only Game in Town…………………... 163

An Unequal Penalty………………..………. 164

The 2017 Highest-Paid Workers...…………. 165

The 2017 Low-Wage Workers:……………... 165

Grandfather Clause Needed…………………. 167

A Low-Income Means Test………………… 168

The Death Benefit & Beneficiaries…………..... 168

Transitional Death Benefits…………………. 169

Stop the Life Expectancy Modification………. 170

Lower the Full Retirement Age……………..…. 171

A COLA Guarantee…………………………. 171

Substantial Earnings, Why 30 Years?………… 172

The State "Match" Trap……………………. 173

An Offset End Date…………………...……... 174

Unobtainable Fixed Returns………………… 176

SS Credits / Contribution Refunds…………… 177

Why a 10-Year Marriage Rule?………………. 178

Motherhood Penalty………………………. 179

Gender Inequality…………………………. 180

Elizabeth Warren…………………...………. 181

COLA for 2017……………...………………. 182

How to contact Treasury Secretary…………… 183

Table of Contents

Chapter 12 – Filing An Appeal........... 185

On Your Own……………….…...…….…….…….. 186

Your Appeal Meeting………………….…..…….. 186

Hearing by Administrative Law Judge…........... 187

Faxes and Registered Mail………………..…..... 188

Unfavorable Decisions……………….….……… 190

Favorable Decisions……………….…...….…….. 191

District Court...……………….……….….…....... 192

Representing Yourself…….………….…….…….. 192

Writing A Brief……………….…………….…… 193

The Section Layout of a Brief……………….……. 193

Certificate of Service……………….……....……... 194

U.S. Circuit Court of Appeals………………....... 194

How to File An Unfair Treatment Complaint.... 195

Advocacy……………………………….….…….. 196

It Only Takes One…………………….….……… 196

About Judge Lyle Douglas Olson……...…….….. 197

Apples vs Oranges………………….…….…….. 199

Not So Fast, Replies The SSA………………....... 199

Appendix A – Government………...…...…….. 201

Appendix B – State Contacts …....…............ 211

Appendix C – Organizations……………....... 219

Appendix D -- Media……...…………..….….... 231

Appendix E – Documents………………...….… 240

INDEX……………………………….………….. 262

About the Author…………………….….…….... 288

Where to Buy This Book………………………... 289

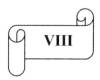

Chapter 1

Overview

𝒯his book is important to you if you are or will be receiving a government pension. Beginning in 2017, thousands of retirees who receive both Social Security (SS) benefits and a government pension will have their pension information downloaded into a computer and matched against current and past Social Security payment records. The SS computers will find retirees who are required to pay offsets, but have not.

Many retirees will receive a snail-mailed letter from the SSA and if you are not exempt, the Social Security Administration, SSA, will demand you return the overpayments. These overpayments, from your unpaid offset penalties, could cost you thousands of dollars. For some retirees, their SS benefits could be stopped until the amount due is recovered.

A Word to the Wise

The purpose of this book is to help you in understanding the different Social Security offset penalties. You will learn how each of the three offsets could affect you; how your offset penalties are calculated; why they are unfair, and how to file an appeal for free. Your understanding of these regulations is important because if you do not know the exact regulation and its code you will find it very difficult when filing your request for an appeal.

The offset regulations may be found in a SSA manual called "POMS," which stands for Program Operations Manual System and is available on the SSA web site.

Covered in detail in this book are the *Windfall Elimination Provision,* the *Government Pension Offset* and the *Dual Entitlement* regulations. This book will save you months of searching for the right regulation and the tedious task of spending weeks combing through and reading thousands of POMS documents.

Knowledge is power and this book will give you the knowledge and the regulation codes you need.

> Focusing exclusively on offset penalties,
>
> this book is a MUST READ if you are
>
> required to pay offset penalties.

In this book you will learn:

the POMS, WEP, GPO and DE regulations

how to file a waiver against SS overpayment penalties

how your monthly offset penalty amount is calculated

the 28 states with state pensions subject to offsets

which workers have offset penalties & those who are exempt

how the SS cuts (modifies) your life expectancy in half

    to double your offset penalties

how you could lose half to all of your SS benefits

why a married spouse could pay two offset penalties

contact information for your state pension agency

how to contact your senators and house representatives

First, a quick overview of the three
offset penalties you face and then
the details of each in the following chapters.

The WEP, GPO and DE Regulations

Civil service workers in 28 states, who are eligible for SS benefits, will pay offset penalties under the Windfall Elimination Provision, WEP. If married or divorced and claiming SS benefits against the earnings account of a spouse or ex-spouse, you will learn how your Government Pension Offset, GPO, will be calculated and applied to your spousal SS benefits. You will not, however, be penalized with both WEP and GPO offsets at the same time.

However, a second offset awaits married retirees, called the Dual Entitlement offset, DE. This offset will be applied along with the GPO penalty, if the retiring spouse applies for Social Security benefits on the earnings record of their spouse or ex-spouse. I am sure it is not surprising to you that many retirees have never heard about these offsets.

States with Offset Penalties

On August 14, 1935, President Franklin D. Roosevelt signed the original Social Security Act. This bill, did not provide SS coverage to civil servants. The reason given was that there were legal questions regarding the Federal government's authority to tax state and local governments.

So, from 1935 to 1954, many states established their own public pension plan which provided civil servants with larger and more generous benefits when they retired.

Each individual district in the 28 states had and still has the option to either switch over to the Social Security System or stay with their state private pension plan. San Diego has adopted a 401(k)-style defined contribution plan. However its retirees will still be subjected to offsets.
www.yahoo.com/news/california-court-upholds-san-diegos-pension-reform-plan-225631762--business.html by Robin Respaut Reuters April 11, 2017

A decision to either stay with the state plan or switch to SS is made by the state district officials and NOT the workers. Because each district within a state could choose to stay with their state's pension plan or switch to SS, district participation in SS became fragmented.

In some states, every district stayed with the state pension plan while in other states almost every district switched over to Social Security. For the districts that switched over to Social Security the decision was irreversible.

The option to switch back to the private state pension, if unsatisfied with the SS system, would NOT be allowed.

In the districts that DID NOT switch over to SS, the civil service employees who will be receiving both a government pension and SS benefits will face offset penalties upon retirement.

The 28 States with Private Pension Systems

Alaska	Kentucky	New Hampshire
California	Louisiana	New Mexico
Colorado	Maine	New York
Connecticut	Massachusetts	Ohio
Florida	Michigan	Pennsylvania
Georgia	Minnesota	Tennessee
Hawaii	Missouri	Texas
Illinois	Montana	Washington
Indiana	Nevada	Wisconsin

Rhode Island (a few districts)

Pension Agency contact information: **Appendix B.**

If you either work or have worked in any of the above 28 states, you could lose from 50% to 100% of your SS benefits, if you will also receive a government pension.

WEP offsets will take up to half of your SS benefits, and the GPO spousal offset could reduce your spousal benefits to zero.

Windfall Elimination Provision - WEP

The Windfall Elimination Provision, WEP, is meant to remove the advantage or "windfall" that the government feels civil servant workers receive from their two pensions. Opponents contend the offsets are imprecise and unfair as these workers earned and paid for their SS benefits.
https://www.fas.org/sgp/crs/.../98-35

If you worked for any employer(s) who did not withhold FICA taxes from your wages, or if you worked in another country, any pension you receive from that work will reduce your Social Security benefits.   Chapter 5, starting on page 47, covers WEP in greater detail.

The Windfall Elimination Provision,

WEP, regulation RS 605.364, will explain

and show you how your Social Security (SS)

offset penalties are calculated.

NOTE: A full printout of this regulation is in Appendix E. page 240

The SSA uses misleading statements in their WEP brochure, stating that the WEP offsets *"may affect, or could affect"* your SS benefits.   If you receive both a Social Security pension and a government pension, there is nothing *"may or could"* about your WEP offset. You will definitely have a WEP offset deducted from your monthly SS pension.   SS WEP brochure No.05-10007 plus Chapter 5

Government Pension Offset - GPO

The Government Pension Offset, GPO, is a Social Security provision that penalizes spouses, or ex-spouses, who apply for Social Security spousal or survivor benefits if they are receiving or will be receiving a private state pension based on their own work.

> **The GPO penalty applies to your SS spousal benefits for any month that you yourself receive a government pension either as a monthly annuity or from a prorated lump-sum payout.**

When you apply for your SS spousal benefits your SS benefit will be reduced by an amount equal to two-thirds of your own monthly government pension. Don't panic -- you will not lose any money from your government pension; the two-thirds is only the number of dollars the SSA will use to reduce your SS benefit. However, the two-thirds deduction could reduce your SS spousal benefits to zero.

S PL 95-216 and GN02608.100   plus Chapter 6

Dual Entitlement Offset - DE

You may be entitled to claim SS benefits on more than one earnings account.   For example, you may be eligible to collect on your own SS earnings record called your *primary insurance account,* PIA, and also on your current or divorced spouses' earnings record.

Your total SS benefit amount will be calculated using the earnings record from the account which will give you the highest benefit. You may choose which account is to be used.   **RS 00615.020 and ssa.gov/poms.nsf/lnx/0300615020**

Dual Entitlement will virtually offset an amount equal to that of the spouse with the lowest SS benefit who collects benefits using the spouse with the larger SS benefits.

For example, if your own SS is $800 and half of your living, spouse's $2,400 SS benefit is $1,200; you could collect on your spouse's larger account.

This means you will keep your $800, but you will collect an additional $400 to equal the $1,200.   Now don't get concerned here either. <u>Your spouse does not lose any of his or her own SS benefits.</u> This amount is only a number, expressed in dollars, that the SSA will use to determine how much more you will receive.

If your spouse were deceased, you would receive your own $800 and the additional $1,600 to bring your total SS benefits to $2,400. In either case, $800 is your offset penalty under DE. If there were no DE, you would receive your $800 plus the full $2,400 for a total of $3,200.

More on DE in Chapter 7

Thanks to President Reagan's 1983 Social Security Refinancing Act, you could easily work all your life and not add one cent more to your SS benefits if you collect upon your spouse's larger PIA.

Program Operations Manual System - POMS

The *Program Operations Manual System,* called POMS, may be found on the SSA web page or by doing a web search using the POMS code letters and numbers assigned to each regulation.

Throughout this book, you will find the POMS codes and an overall view of the most important features in each regulation. The POMS regulations in this book were current as of Nov. I, 2017. However, these regulations are occasionally changed so you may want to do a web search for the newest version.

When Congress passes a regulation, the President may reject it or sign it into law. Only Congress can write, amend, and request that the President repeal these POMS regulations.

The courts and the judges do not write, amend, or repeal offset regulations. In an appeals case, the judge only reviews the regulations to verify that they have been correctly applied.

When you search the *ssa.gov* website and scroll to *Policy Home Section C,* you will read the following statement:

> **"The public version of POMS is identical to the version used by Social Security employees EXCEPT that it does NOT include internal data entry and sensitive content instructions."**

This means that the Social Security web page restricts you from viewing the full version of a POMS regulation. However, you may read the *FULL VERSION* of each regulation using the code and doing a web search.

The Social Security Act of 1935

The basic SS program provides *insurance protection* for the worker, the spouse, ex-spouses, and the children.

Eric Kingson, a professor at Syracuse University, said,

"The premiums that we pay are designed to insure against the risk of lost wages due to the retirement or death of the family provider."

The benefits are not based upon need. Instead, the wage earner must meet the requirement of 40 quarters of work in his or her lifetime, in a job(s) where he or she paid FICA taxes.

In 2018, a worker will need $1,320 of SS covered wages in a quarter to have it count. A typical quarter is January 1 to March 31.

www.ssa.gov/pubs/EN-05-10035.pdf

Operating now for 80 years, Social Security provides money to those eligible who are unemployed, disabled, a spouse, an ex-spouse(s), retirees who receive Social Security and Medicare benefits and the children of a deceased worker. A worker pays for this social "insurance" with the FICA taxes deducted from his or her wages.

Your SS benefit will be calculated, using your highest 35 years of earnings, where you paid Social Security FICA taxes. If you have less than the 35 years, you will receive a zero for the years without SS covered wages.

> ## Social Security benefits are NOT gratuities, they are NOT handouts and they are NOT charity.
>
> ## SS benefits are an EARNED RIGHT based upon an individual's contributions and earnings.
>
> ## The individual has earned the right, to receive their SS benefits in dignity and self-respect.
>
> Court case FLEMMING V. NESTOR 363 U.S. 603.
> www.ssa.gov/history/nestor.html *102 Cong. Rec. 15110*

All wages earned until you turn 60 years of age are indexed (increased) for inflation. The wages one earns after age 60 will not be indexed, but they will be considered when the SSA chooses your highest 35 SS earning years. Today, sixty million Americans receive SS benefits. For many, the SS benefits are their sole source of income.

The *Federal Insurance Contributions Act*, FICA, taxes are deposited in the *Federal Old-Age and Survivors Insurance Trust Fund.* Only the workers who contribute to the fund, including their spouse, ex-spouse(s) and children, are entitled to its benefits if eligible.

See: 42 U.S.C. 401(a) and Title 26, Subtitle C, Chapter 21 USC   and
Chapter 8 covers in detail the Trust Fund and its investments.

President Reagan

President Reagan said, "*Government is the problem.*" Eager to please his contributors, whose money was very generously donated to his campaign, he began an unrelenting attack upon what he called "entitlements." The word, "entitlements," is used to give one the impression that Social Security is either welfare or a handout paid with taxpayers' dollars. Nothing could be further from the truth.

The Congressional Representatives and the media use the demeaning name, "entitlements," when talking about SS retiree benefits. This creates resentment among current workers, who have heard that SS may go bankrupt.

During Reagan's first term, the nation fell into a recession. While Federal spending grew, the degree of income inequality in America widened substantially.   One of Reagan's most controversial, early moves was to fire most of the nation's air traffic controllers, who took part in a strike.   Unfortunately, Reagan then signed the offset regulations into law and reduced Social Security for both disabled individuals and the survivors of deceased workers.   wikipedia.org/wiki/Presidency of Ronald Reagan

A criticism of Reagan's policies was that they created a situation, in which the rich became richer, while the poor became poorer. Reagan believed that excessive regulations and social programs hampered the American economy. Despite his indicated belief, he signed even more regulations into law with the POMS offset penalties.

Anger and resentment now exists among current workers who are aware, that government retirees with a government pension are also filing for a Social Security pension. These current workers feel they are paying FICA taxes towards a SS pension they may never see. This propaganda is extremely effective in pitting current workers and retired citizens against one another, rather than fighting the problem of inadequate SS benefits.

Commissioner of SS -- Job Description

"The Commissioner of Social Security shall have full power and authority to make rules and regulations and to establish procedures......"

Sec. 205 [U.S.C. 405] (a) Compilation of the Social Security Laws - Evidence, Procedure, and Certification for Payment.

Congress has granted the commissioner the power to interpret the regulations, as he or she alone understands them. The commissioner has sole authority, without a congressional vote, to write rules, regulations, and procedures and is able to easily overturn legal decisions by claiming that there was an *"error in law."*

I'll bet you're wondering why we should bother to have a congressional vote or have the President sign the regulations into law if the Commissioner alone can rewrite each regulation. I am also wondering about the commissioners' unlimited power.

To taint the perception of the public, politicians and the media refer to Social Security as an "entitlement" and to government retirees as "undeserving" and "old, greedy geezers."

However, the facts tell a different story as explained in the following book,

Social Security Works,

by N.J. Altman and E.R. Kingson

Chapter 2

Private State Pensions

Employees Facing Offsets

𝒮he **largest group with government** pensions is the teachers in the K-12 public schools and the professors working in the state colleges. This group also includes bus drivers, janitors, school nurses, school lunch workers, office staff, coaches, principals, department directors, administrators, etc.

Others who are affected are the state, city, and local workers in the water, sewer, street, police and fire departments; city office and library employees; state, and city park employees; local airport staff; and all temporary, part-time or seasonal workers in these departments.

If you ever worked in a government civil service position in a state, which had a private pension plan, you will face offset penalties if you are eligible for both a government pension and a SS pension.

The Private Pension

The private pension plan, in most states, will give retirees two choices:

1. **Lump Sum** -- the lump-sum payout will usually return all of your contributions along with your share of the capital gains on the investments made by the pension agency.

2. **Annuity** – the most popular, is the annuity with monthly payments for the rest of your life.

> I highly recommended you opt for
> the annuity if given a choice.

If you are in poor health, or have a short life expectancy, then you may want to take the lump-sum option. Retirees who meet certain eligibility requirements may also receive fully paid health insurance and the option to add a beneficiary.

Beneficiaries – Be Careful

You must be careful with your choice of a beneficiary, since in many plans, it is a permanent choice. If later on, you want to change your beneficiary, you may find you will not be allowed to do so.

You could postpone your choice of a beneficiary, since in many plans, you can add a beneficiary at any time even after you retire. When you choose a beneficiary, both you and your future benefactor, in most cases, will receive a reduced monthly benefit.

Should you marry, without having added a beneficiary, you will have a short time frame, perhaps only a month or two, to add your new spouse as a beneficiary. However, each plan has different options, so do not assume anything. Always check with your pension agency to learn which options are available in your state pension plan.

FICA Taxes

Taxes under the *Federal Insurance Contributions Act, FICA,* combines the Social Security Old Age, Survivors, Disability and Unemployment Tax, and the Medicare health insurance tax.

In 2018, 175 million workers will pay FICA taxes, while 42 million retirees will receive Social Security benefits.

The FICA rate for 2018 is 7.65% and is a combination of the 6.2% SS tax and the 1.45% Medicare tax on wages up to $128,400.   www.ssa.gov/oact/cola

---

In 2016, half of all workers, over 86 million, earned $31,099 or less.

Only <u>six</u> out of a hundred workers are considered high-paid employees earning $128,400 per year or more.

www.ssa.gov/cgi-bin/netcomp.cgi?year=2017

The maximum FICA tax in 2018 is $19,645.20 with $9,822.60 paid by the worker and $9,822.60 paid by the employer. Once the high-paid worker reaches $128,400 in wages, he or she and he or she's employer will no longer pay the FICA SS tax.

You can see how these high earners, no longer paying FICA SS taxes, can easily afford to save, and contribute to either a retirement account and/or a 401(k). However, the average low-paid worker, still paying FICA taxes, finds saving or investing in a retirement account a luxury.

www.nasi.org/learn/socialsecurity/who-pays
www.mybudget360.com/how-much-do-americans-earn-in-2017

Social Security Eligibility

If you worked in one or more Social Security covered positions and accumulated forty quarters, you will be eligible, upon retirement, for Social Security benefits. A quarter is three months with four quarters in a calendar year. A typical quarter is January through March; April through June, etc. Your forty quarters do not need to be earned in a single continuous period.

Many of you may have worked part-time where you paid FICA taxes. As a Social Security covered employee, your wages will count toward one or more Social Security quarters. Social Security covered wages of at least $1,320, earned during any part of a three-month period in 2018, will count as one quarter.

No Refunds

Your FICA contributions for Social Security and Medicare insurance are *non-refundable*. You have only one SS option and that is the monthly annuity. Your benefit amount will be calculated using the wages credited to your own *Primary Insurance Account*, PIA, or your spouse's PIA account, whichever one gives you the largest benefit. You may choose the account you prefer to use. However, do not make the mistake of being too hasty; there are other options to consider before you apply for benefits.

Social Security Options

By delaying retirement or using the correct PIA, you have a one-time opportunity to increase your SS benefits. Any increase in your monthly benefit could produce thousands of dollars for you over your lifetime. You really need to know all your options and the consequences of each.

You may want to read, *Get What's Yours* by Lawrence Kotlikoff. This book, available at most libraries and on Amazon.com, is one of the best books on the various strategies you can use to maximize your SS benefits.

www.amazon.com/Get-Whats-Yours.../147677   info in Appendix D p.235

Another great source of Social Security information is a book by Attorney Joseph Matthews, called *Social Security, Medicare & Government Pensions (22nd edition)*. This book is available in most libraries, on Amazon & from the web site, **www.nolo.com.**   the 23rd edition will be available around March 2018

Average SS Benefits

The average monthly benefit in 2017 for all females 65 and older, was $1,231.50 and for men, 65 and older, it averaged $1,583.77.

Full retirement age in 2018 for those

born in 1956 is age 66 and 4 months.

with a maximum benefit of $2,788.

www.ssa.gov/policy/docs/chartbooks/fast_facts/2017
www.ssa.gov/policy/docs   SSS Pub. No. 13-11785

Repeatedly, we have been told that Social Security benefits were not intended to be our sole source of income in retirement.   However, most workers do not plan for retirement until well into their 40's or 50's. With company pensions quickly disappearing, workers in low-paying positions are at risk.

These workers seldom have a 401(k) plan and only a few have an Individual Retirement Account, IRA. With only a few years left before retiring, their savings, if any, will not be adequate.

Unprepared retirees may experience constant anxiety, knowing that they are vulnerable and worry about the day when they cannot pay their bills. Today, it is common to find retirees among the growing, homeless population. It is unfair for our government to penalize these struggling retirees with offsets.

www.jec.senate.gov/public/_cache/files/0f433655-7d45-4313-aa50-f4b7864d2a20/social-security-and-retirement-savings-in-the-united-states-final.pdf

.

Currently, the regulations do not grandfather anyone out of these offsets. No one is exempt, regardless of his or her income. Without a "means" test, the poor are trapped, as their small Social Security check is decreased even further by an offset penalty.

With U.S. tax dollars being sent overseas to help the "poor" in other countries, it is a travesty that our own poor are left to struggle with WEP, GPO and DE offset penalties, robbing them of their meager SS benefits.

State Contact Information

See Appendix B for agency contact information for each of the 28 states with a private pension plan.

If you have additional or different information, please email it to: ssoffsets@yahoo.com

Chapter 3

Saving Social Security

𝒻anning the public's fear of the SS facing the possibility of a shortage of funds, congress and the moneyed, special interest groups, have been hammering relentlessly about "saving" Social Security.

The 1983-Refinancing Act

President Reagan and congress amended the Social Security Act of 1935 with the *1983 SS Refinancing Act,* changing the benefit eligibility for public employees, making it legal for the SSA to deny civil service retirees their SS benefits. The Act caught many workers in the middle of their careers, unaware of how devastating the offset penalties would be on their SS benefits.

The Act unfairly singles out public retirees and severely penalizes the low-income retirees, while eliminating offsets for those who had earned large incomes. SS is a retiree's financial safety net. However, the net has been removed from under civil servants, allowing some of the poorest government retirees to drop into poverty.

Public retirees are the sacrificial scapegoats in the Refinancing Act. They are vilified as "greedy takers" and are required to show they have had substantial SS earnings for thirty years before they can receive 100% of their SS benefits. This qualifying hurdle is only required of civil service workers who receive a government pension. To learn how much you need to earn each year to have the year count as a substantial earnings credit, go to the SS web site: www.ssa.gov/pubs/10045.html

Social Security is Not Going Bankrupt

With over a *three trillion dollar* surplus, which is growing every year, SS is unlikely to go bankrupt anytime soon. Despite frequent claims that the SS Trust Fund is "going broke," the latest SS Trustees' report maintains that even if no action is taken to shore up the program, it will pay full benefits through 2034, according to the *U.S. Congress Joint Economic Committee* report dated August, 2016.

www.jec.senate.gov/public/_cache/files 9/2016

Your Benefit Statements

The shocking, eye-opening nightmare unfolds when the retiree applies for Social Security. Most retirees will receive far less than what their SS benefit statements indicated. SS benefit statements, mailed to them for years by the SSA, failed to warn them about offset penalties.

Retirees usually learn about their offset penalties from the SS clerk, who has the unpleasant task of telling the retiree how many dollars will be deducted from his or her SS check.

While the WEP reduction is limited to no more than 50% of your own earned SS benefits, the GPO offset deduction for a married or divorced spouse is unlimited. The spouse may lose every cent of his or her spousal SS benefits.

Substantial Earnings

The substantial earnings requirement is not only upside-down and regressive, but also favors highly paid workers. The disadvantaged poor, without substantial earnings, receive some of the lowest SS benefits and pay the highest offset penalties.

The SSA feels that it has solved the *unfairness* problem by reducing or eliminating the offset deductions for those with 20 to 30 years of *substantial* SS covered earnings.

Although highly paid workers easily meet the yearly, substantial earnings requirement, not everyone has had a steady job with a large paycheck. Many jobs are sporadic, with some years generating large, but temporary incomes, followed by sparse earnings or unemployment. Oil field workers; farmers; and those who work in a trade such as painters, carpenters, heavy equipment operators, seasonal workers; and many others repeatedly swing from feast to famine.

The years which show your SS earnings credits as zero, may be due to you're taking time off for childcare, elderly parent care giving, health issues, or lack of work.

Without the total lifetime of wages averaged, many workers will fail to reach even the lowest substantial earnings minimum of twenty years.

The current, outdated, offset-penalty formula sets the substantial earnings requirement so high that minimum wage and low-income workers seldom qualify.

Many highly paid workers with 30 years of substantial SS earnings will NOT pay offset penalties.

To find out how large a penalty percentage you will pay go to
the chart found on the following SSA web site:
www.ssa.gov/planners/retire/wep-chart.html

Why has congress not set an offset percentage rate that is the same for everyone?

Why should your income decide your offset rate?

A retiree's failure to appeal may be because he or she does not know that the SS appeals are free. He or she may not know either how or where to appeal, or which POMS regulation is causing the SS offset penalty.

See Chapter 12 for information on how to appeal.

Who Gets Hurt?

Women and minorities are hurt the most. The uncompromising SSA exempts no one and does not offer options. The SS does not consider that it is nearly impossible for women and minorities to obtain the required years of substantial earnings when our culture has paid them less money, limited their job opportunities, and expected the woman to be the stay-at-home caretaker.

Our government creates pages of reports and statistical analyses on the disparity in wages for women and minorities as compared to white men, yet allows employers to pay women and minorities less money for similar work.

Life is unfair, but our government could make a greater effort toward correcting the inequities in the substantial earnings formula by reducing both the wages and the years required for women and minorities to qualify.

The Offset Gauntlet

Nevertheless, why should any retiree have to run this gauntlet of POMS regulations, whose sole purpose is to withhold his or her SS benefits? You worked and paid the FICA taxes. You earned your Social Security insurance.

**Your benefits are NOT based on need;
they are NOT welfare and
they are NOT a free handout.**

You were told that if you met the SSA eligibility requirements, you would receive x-number of dollars in benefits. This promise has turned out to be a lie and has ruined many retirees' lives.

> **How can anyone in our government look**
> **a retiree in the face and not be ashamed**
> **of the way that the SSA is treating**
> **the civil servants in this country?**

The SSA Guarantee

The SS guarantees that it will take only half of your own SS benefits under the WEP regulations. How about that for a guarantee? *Only half*! We are so blessed!

However, this guarantee does NOT include the GPO marriage penalty nor the spousal DE penalty.

"The law protects (??) you if you get a low pension. We will not reduce your Social Security benefits by more than *HALF* of your pension for earnings after 1956 on which you did not pay Social Security taxes."

SS Pub #05-10045

Such a deal! The law protects you.

Really? They sure had me fooled.

Somehow, I didn't feel "protected."

How Propaganda Fuels the Jealousy

With its propaganda of shortages, the SSA uses fear as a weapon to encourage young voters to vote for those who would "fix" Social Security by increasing the retirement age, cutting benefits, and/or increasing FICA taxes.

It's disturbing to hear about this emotional
terrorism aimed at influencing the
votes and thinking of our young people.

The SSA demonizes government retirees by insinuating that current retirees are draining the SS Trust Fund dry. The SS also lets the public falsely assume that if a retiree receives a government pension, he or she has no right to collect his or her earned SS benefits. These negative messages create anger and resentment in the minds of current workers.

One thing is certain. The offsets will not stop any time soon. You're stuck, without a low-income exemption; without a grandfather clause; and with an outdated, one-size-fits-all offset formula, favoring highly paid, white male workers.

Your only option is to cry, as hundreds of your hard-earned and badly needed SS retirement dollars are withheld from you each month.

Intimidated by the SSA and
without knowledge
of the POMS regulations,
most retirees
say nothing
and do nothing.

A few appeal.

The old divide-and-conquer system is still
operating, as each retiree, who files an appeal,
fights the SSA alone.

You have not only been deceived for years,
but when you retire, you are
expected to accept it.

Where are our

Senators?

Where are our

Representatives?

Why are they not

objecting to,

revising,

or repealing

these ugly, unfair offsets?

Chapter 4

Notification

*A*fter **January 1, 2005, each state** with a private pension plan was required to notify its government employees about the SS offset penalties. Prior to 2005, workers were left clueless, while the irresponsible SSA dragged its feet from 1983 until 2004, a full 21 years, before the *Social Security Protection Act,* SSPA, mandated that all private pension agencies must notify current and new hires about SS offsets.   SSPA Public Law #108-203 & POMS RS 01505.001
www.library.clerk.house.gov/reference-files /PPL_108_203

<u>Confused SS Staff & Confused Retiree</u>

Although you have been "notified" by your employer about potential offsets, you may still be confused about the offset penalties due to the vague wording in the POMS regulations. You may begin to feel like a ping-pong ball as each SS clerk arrives at a different explanation and dollar amount for your offset penalty. In many cases, the SS representative cannot figure out which offset regulation to apply or even if you should have an offset. With so many conflicting answers to the same question, it is impossible to know which answer is right.

A hearing held on May 21, 1998, before the *Subcommittee on Social Security*, surfaced many of the contradictory and poorly written regulations. However, it is still Greek to most of us and the SS explanations are about as clear as mud.

House Hearing, 105 Congress, Second Session Serial 105-49

A separate *U.S. General Accounting Office* (GAO) study indicated that the SSA office clerks are often unable to determine whether or not a retiree should have the WEP or GPO applied.

WEP reduces your tier one SS benefits from 90% down to 40% of your actual yearly wages. Opponents say that the 40% benefit factor is arbitrary, inaccurate, imprecise and regressive. Thus it over penalizes both low-paid workers with short careers or full time workers with careers split between the public and private sectors. Tiers are on page 165.

In a 1998 hearing, *Chairman Jim Bunning of Kentucky*, said to *Ms. Cynthia M. Fagnoni, Director of the U.S. General Accounting Office, GAO:*

"The offsets seemed fair at the time of enactment." Then Jim Bunning asked Ms. Fagnoni, Do you feel that the offsets are fair now?

Ms. Fagnoni replied,

"What our report really shows is how difficult those provisions are to administer."

She went on to say,

"The provisions are so complicated that it's difficult for the SSA to check on all of their clerks to see if they're applying the GPO/WEP offsets correctly."

The Offset Fights

During another hearing held on May 21, 1998, before the *Subcommittee on Social Security, William Jefferson, CA-D,* proposed limiting the offsets to only those with SS benefits that exceed $2000, while *Pete Stark, CA-D*, proposed that the GPO offsets be reduced from two-thirds to one-third of a retiree's state pension. Both proposals were defeated.

www.congress.gov/congression-report/105th-congress/house

Ranking Member Robert T. Matsui, CA-D, agreed in saying, a "Review of the entire policy may be needed. He stressed "House bill H.R. 743 was designed to address many issues beyond the GPO provision. The merit of the overall package should override objections to Section 418." Strong opposition to the GPO, section 418, revision ensued from *Ruben Hinojosa, TX-D, Solomon Ortiz, TX-D.* As a result, nothing was changed.

ssa.gov/policy/docs/ssb/v68n4/v68n4p41.html

Kevin Brady and Richard Neal H.R. 711

House bill H.R. 711, entitled "*Equal Treatment of Public Servants Act of 2015*," was a bill sponsored by *Mr. Kevin Brady, TX-R*, and *Mr. Richard Neal, MA-D.* On July 13, 2016, Brady said the bill would be tabled for now because "public servants are not in agreement about this legislation." Brady went on to say, "Over 1.7 million people are subject to the WEP's flawed benefit calculation formula, which can reduce their Social Security benefits by over $400 a month."

> *"We need the community to come together on*
> *what they can all support or the consequence,*
> *unfortunately, is to see the current*
> *WEP harm people on a daily basis*
> *that frankly don't deserve being harmed."*
>
> Kevin Brady   July 13, 2015   H.R. Bill 711

Brady then went on to say:

"It never seemed fair to me that public servants, who earn a pension at work and also in Social Security, whether it was a second job, summer job, or a second career, should be docked Social Security benefits.

He also said that these workers teach our children, keep us safe, and race to our rescue when in need. Brady said, *The Equal Treatment for Public Servants Act* would have repealed the current WEP and put in place a formula that is more fair by calculating benefits using a teacher's, firefighter's, or police officer's actual earnings history. This bill is about getting equal treatment for public servants."

www.fedsmith.com/2016/07/13/HR 711

Three Big Mistakes

It is evident that not every law congress creates works as it was intended. The WEP, GPO, and DE offset regulations are three examples; they are three big mistakes. Offsets are predatory, snaring retired workers at a time in their lives when they are the most vulnerable and robbing them of their pension benefits when they can least afford the loss.

Although the SS appeals are free, if the retiree hires an attorney, the retiree is expected to foot the bill. This costly obstacle stops many retirees from appealing. However, if your income is low enough, you may qualify for free legal assistance, as long as you are willing to answer questions regarding your personal finances.

Some retirees appeal their SS offset determination, while others just accept the offset deductions without question. Those who do appeal are often run over by the juggernaut of SS attorneys and judges, who are reluctant to reverse or question the decisions of the SS commissioner.

While the retiree must pay to fight if he or she hires an attorney, the SSA has plenty of money. Oops, I mean that the SSA has our SS money to pay the salaries of the SSA's legal team. This money comes from your FICA tax contributions to the SS Trust Fund.

How to file an appeal without an attorney- see Chapter 12.

Need to Know Basis

Employers seem to provide you with the critical offset notification on a "need to know" basis, only after you have been hired which is far too late. Today, although you may receive more information about offsets, the information is usually skimpy and vague.

Of course, if your potential employer informed you thoroughly about your future SS offset penalties, you may have taken a second look at the job offer. Perhaps you would have requested a larger salary to replace the SS benefits you would lose to offset penalties.

Remember the WEP, GPO, and DE offsets will take hundreds of dollars every month from you and your spouse for the rest of your lives. However, by the time you learn about the SS offset penalties, you may have already accepted the new job, having perhaps given a "last day" notice to your employer. If you have reached this point, you are behind the eight ball, making it hard for you to turn back.

SS Fantasy – A Reality Check

The government claims that those affected by the *1983 Refinancing Act* had ample time to alter their retirement plans and careers. This may be true for younger workers, but changing one's career late in life is a SSA fantasy, which seldom works in the real world. How much time is ample time anyway?

The reality is that good jobs are hard to find when you are an older worker with obsolete, or job specific skills. Employers, who hire older workers, usually pay low wages. Many seniors find that the better paying positions are physically too demanding.

In many cases, workers in their 50's and 60's are established. They may own a home, or not be willing to move. It takes a lifetime for a person to become rooted, gather friends, and become a member of a community. Establishing professional credibility, clients, or patients takes years, something one will lose if one relocates.

Other family members may also factor into the job relocation decision. Children may not want to leave their school or their friends. A spouse may also have a job that cannot be easily replaced. Uprooting and moving may be just too difficult. Reality sets in as the "ample-time" to change your career runs out.

Would you ever advise anyone to become a public school teacher, a police officer, librarian, or fire fighter knowing he or she would face severe SS offset penalties?

Would you or anyone you know want to move to a new and different state?

You're probably thinking, "NO."

How our government penalizes our public servants is reprehensible. Why the SSA waited until 2004 before it mandated all public employees receive SS offset notification is even more puzzling. In any case, it is time for Congress to repeal the existing financially ruinous, offset penalties.

The Elephant in the Room

The SSA does not see offsets as a problem. Offsets are only a problem for you and me. The offset status quo works great for the SSA. It fattens its coffers, so why change a good thing? Why would congress or the commissioner want to stop the offset gravy train arriving at the SS Trust Fund gate every month, full of unpaid benefits, legally withheld from retirees.

While many petitions and suggestions have been presented to the SSA by the NEA, the SS Fairness, and many other groups, the unfair offsets, have not been changed.

www.NEA.org
The National Education Association is the largest labor union.
www.ssfairness.com.
For other organizations and groups see Appendix D page 219

In the past, commissioners seemed unconcerned with the annoying complaints from us, the little people and tone-deaf to the voices asking that the WEP, GPO and DE regulations be revised or repealed.

In the meantime, the majority of the
members of Congress ignore the
elephant in the room.

When SS clerks are repeatedly making errors after thirty-plus years of offset regulations, and experienced judges are making simple "errors in the law," it's time to have the POMS regulations simplified. If the application of a POMS regulation is vague and confusing, Congress should rewrite the regulation to clarify the exact, intended meaning, rather than having angry retirees appealing the same questionable offset regulations again and again.

> *It's time for Congress to acknowledge that*
>
> *there is an*
>
> ## ELEPHANT IN THE ROOM.
>
> *Congress needs to get **RID** of it!*

In the past commissioners appeared to be incapable of understanding the offset problems, which have plagued the SSA for years. Even with only a seemingly vague understanding of the offset laws, the commissioner has the power to write regulations. His or her failure, to request that congress rewrite or repeal these offsets, shows a lack of empathy for struggling retirees.

On January 23, 2017, Nancy Berryhill
became the new acting commissioner.
Hopefully we may finally see
the offsets repealed.

Retirees and current workers

expect strong leadership from

their appointed SSA commissioners.

However, during the last 30 years,

the commissioners have been

very disappointing.

Chapter 5

Windfall Elimination Provision

$\mathcal{T}$he Social Security Amendments of *1983* introduced the *Windfall Elimination Provision, WEP,* as a way of eliminating the "*windfall*" of Social Security benefits received by retirees who also receive a government pension. The purpose of WEP is to <u>equalize</u> public retirees with their peers who receive only Social Security.

web search   Public Law 98-21

The SSA applies a WEP offset penalty to retirees who split their working career between Social Security covered jobs and government civil service positions in states with a private pension system.These retired government workers, which do NOT include the military and federal workers, are called "*double-dippers.*" This demeaning name is meant to shame them and make civil servants feel guilty for requesting their Social Security benefits.

The WEP regulations give the SSA the legal authority to penalize these public retirees, and thereby causing tragic and unintended consequences.   **7-5700 www.crs.gov. 98-35**

> **Of the 60 million receiving Social Security benefits in 2016, only *1.4 million or 4 percent* have been singled out for the WEP offset penalties.**
>
> 2016/fast_facts16.pdf

The Windfall Logic

The WEP offset formula is based on flawed logic, because it assumes that you are receiving more than you should from your two pensions, which is not logically possible. The one thing I know for certain, is that you can only be working and earning retirement credits in one pension system at a time.

When you work x-number of hours in a civil position, your government pension receives your contributions. The same is true for Social Security. The hours you work in a SS covered job where you pay FICA taxes are credited to your SS account.

Your pension contributions go toward one pension system or the other, never both. Therefore, you receive only the pension benefits that you earned in each system. The combined pensions equal 100% of your total retirement income. The following perhaps explains this concept a little more clearly.

If you own two cars, you can only drive one at a time. Therefore, mileage will accumulate only on the car you are currently driving. If you decide to drive a second car, this second car only will accumulate mileage. You cannot accumulate mileage on both cars at the same time.

The combined total mileage you drive in your lifetime is allocated among all the cars you have driven, with each car contributing a fraction of the total miles. When all of the miles are added together, you have a total of 100%.

The SS and state private pension plans accumulate benefits in a similar manner. The SSA, however, feels that because you receive both a government pension and Social Security benefits, you are receiving a *"windfall."* Therefore, your benefits need to be *"equalized"* (reduced).

This "*equalization*" means that you are penalized with offsets on your SS pension to reduce your total combined pension benefit income to be equal to the small, inadequate SS benefits (income) paid to your peers.

Rather than solving the problem of inadequate SS benefits, the SSA's logic is to use offsets to reduce the retirement income of a civil servant by lowering his or her SS benefits. The logical solution to this problem is that the SS needs to increase the benefits of the SS retirees and "equalize" them with their government peers who have larger state pensions.

Public Pension Payment Options

In most states, government retirees have two payment options, they may take a lump sum or an annuity. However, many states require that you take the lump sum payout if you worked less than five years. Your monthly offset dollar deductions are similar, regardless of which option you select.

Those who take the annuity have a WEP offset of 2/3rds of their monthly government pension deducted from their monthly SS benefit. However, this deduction is limited to no more than 50% of his or her monthly SS benefit. Those who take the lump sum option will have their monthly offset deductions calculated by the SSA office.

In both the lump sum and the annuity, the WEP offset, based on your own SS earnings record is limited to no more than 50% of your monthly SS benefit. This 50% limit, however, is misleading. It is not the monthly amount that is wrong, but the fact that it goes on and on forever. This clever, mathematical illusion in the WEP regulations, will siphon 100% of your government pension back into the SS Trust Fund by repeatedly deducting the full pension amount over again and again.

On top of this deduction, you could pay a second offset penalty, called "Dual Entitlement," DE. This additional DE offset will activate if you file for SS benefits on either your living or deceased spouse's SS earnings record, rather than your own SS account.

How did Congress arrive at 50% for WEP offsets? They just picked a percentage and made it law.

Specific Time Period

In *POMS RS 00605.364, Section C* is a very important policy. It says the SSA would "*stop all further offsets after the specific time period ends, but ONLY if the paying agency provided the prorated monthly amount.*"

POMS 00605.364

**Determining Pension Applicability Eligibility
Date, and Monthly Amount - Section C # 5**

When the entire pension is paid in a lump sum, the amount may represent a   payment for a specific period of time or a "lifetime."

Generally, the pension- paying agency will prorate the lump sum to determine a monthly amount for WEP purposes.

If the agency does not provide this information, (SSA will) prorate the lump sum to determine the monthly pension amount as follows:

Specific Period - *Divide the lump sum by the   number of months in the period specified by the pension-paying agency.*

See RS 00605.360C.5.a. when WEP application ends.

Lifetime or Unspecified Period - *Divide the pension lump sum amount by the appropriate actuarial value in the table that corresponds to the worker's age on the date of the lump sum award.*

See RS 00605.360C.5.a. when WEP application ends.

A full version of RS 605.364 is in Appendix E

Many pension-paying agencies will neither provide a

specific time period nor a prorated monthly amount.

The agency then leaves your private pension

exposed to offset exploitation by the SSA.

In the 2014 SS memorandum, *A-09-13-2304, 9,* you will find the following very important statement:

> *"The SSA must prorate the lump sum payment*
> *over a beneficiary's expected lifetime.*
> *The SSA considers the beneficiary's life*
> *expectancy and age at the time of the award*
> *to prorate the lump sum payment*
> *into a monthly amount."*

This memorandum does not mention that the SSA
would "modify" your life expectancy.
Oig.ssa.gov/.../A-09-13-23049.pdf 5/27/2014

The *POMS 605.364* regulation shows that the SS allows *ONLY the pension paying agency* to determine your prorated amount and ending date. If the state agency fails to provide this date, it is classified as an *"Unspecified Period."* The SSA commissioner then has the congressional approved authority to decide your monthly prorated deductions (dollar amount) by using your "modified" life expectancy.

<u>The Question is WHY?</u> Why is the paying agency given this exclusive privilege when anyone with a calculator can determine the length of time and the ending date of his or her lump sum by dividing it by the value next to his or her age in the "Modified Lifetime Chart?"

It is even more puzzling as to why the state agencies refuse to provide the ending date and the prorated dollar amount. If the SSA can determine the prorated amount, so can the state agency. Instead retirees are thrown to the hungry, pension-devouring, SSA offset wolves.

I would like to know where I could find the law that made the pension paying agency the *sole* decision maker when it comes to prorating a lump sum!

It also makes you wonder what the Actuarial Life Table actually is. Is it the lifetime of a lump sum (of money) or a person's life expectancy?

In his decision, ALJ Judge Olson wrote that the chart was the "lifetime of a lump sum."   However, the SSA commissioner claims that the POMS 605.364 *"Lifetime Table of Actuarial Values"* is your modified "life expectancy and not the lifetime of your lump sum."   The SSA's viewpoint may be found online in the legal brief filed in court by the SSA. Use the following to locate it on the internet:

Tenth Circuit Court of Appeals, Docket No. 13-1542, pages 12 & 13

As you can see, there are two different opinions with two very different outcomes, one favoring the retiree and the other favoring the SSA.

Your "Modified" Life Expectancy

Your monthly offset amount is determined by dividing your lump sum by your expected life expectancy, LE. The mathematical illusion begins with the Table of Actuarial Values found in the *POMS RS 00605.364* regulation. When you read this regulation, you may think that what is implied is obvious, but you will learn in the next paragraphs, that it is not.

Immediately, you will notice the "lifetime table" does not differentiate between men and women. In contrast, a "real" life expectancy table has different life-expectancy values for men and women.

I have placed these two charts together so you can see for yourself the disparity between the SSA's "modified life expectancy" and what your real life expectancy actually is. Both charts are produce by the SSA, and may be found on their *ssa.gov* web site, which begs the question:

Why are the following charts so different?

"Modified" Lifetime Chart (altered)

Your "fake life expectancy" in months

Use your age and the date when you took your lump sum.

POMS 00605.364

Age	Award Date After 6/1/2016	Award Date 6/1/11 - 5/31/16	Award Date 6/1/07 - 5/31/11	Award Date 5/31/07 or before
55	216.8	155.6	151.5	**140.9***
60	193.5	142.8	138.4	127.2
65	168.4	128.4	123.8	112.1
70	142.4	112.2	107.8	96.7

- * 140.9 months equals 11.74 years

Your "Real" (actual) Life Expectancy

Period Life Table for those retiring before 2013

Age	Males		Females	
	YEARS	MONTHS	YEARS	MONTHS
55	25.41	304.90	**28.74**	**344.9**
60	21.48	257.76	24.46	293.52
65	17.75	213.00	20.32	243.84
70	14.24	170.88	16.43	197.1

www.ssa.gov/oact/STATS/table4c6.html 2013

Full versions of these charts begin on pages 240 and 255.

You may spend your lump sum in a year or use the funds only when you need extra cash. Regardless of how you spend your lump sum, it will not change how the SSA calculates your monthly offset amount.

The *POMS RS 00605.364 C (5a) policy,* states:

"The WEP computation is no longer used when the entitlement to the pension payment ceases or the <u>*proration of a lump sum payment ends*</u>.

The recomputation is effective the first month for which the claimant is no longer entitled to the pension."

Sounds good, but I do not know of anyone who has had their offset deductions stopped and their SS benefits fully restored.

Your Real Life Expectancy

Using the "real" actual life expectancy table, you see that a woman, age 55, (yes, different values for males and females) could be expected to live 28.74 years, or 344.9 months but, in the *"Modified" or Fake Lifetime Chart,* her LE was reduced to 11.74 years or 140.9 months.

SS Actuarial REAL Life Tables, 2013 page 56

We immediately notice that her fake "modified" LE cheated her out of 204 months (344.9 - 140.9). The way in which Social Security doubles your offset penalty is by reducing your LE causing the offset dollars deducted from your SS check to be doubled or even tripled each month.

www.ssa.gov/oact/STATS/table4c6.html

Over time, the total SS offset deductions will double or even triple the amount of her original government lump sum or annuity pension.

For example:

If we divide her imaginary $30,000 lump sum by her "modified" fake LE of 140.9 months, we arrive at a monthly offset of $212.92. However, if we divide the $30,000 by her "real" actual life expectancy of 344.9 months, we learn that her monthly offset deduction should actually be $86.98 per month. She is overpaying $125.93 per month.

In 30 years, when she is 85, the offsets will have cost her $76,650, which is over 2½ times the $30,000 she received. The SSA assumes that most retirees will not do the math. This assumption is right, as few have. This doubled-plus, offset penalty grab is a big "windfall" for the SSA.

The workers, at age 55, who take their lump sum on June 1, 2016 or after will receive an extra 76 months. Meanwhile, those who retired before 2007 have been overlooked, ignored, and forgotten. They will receive no adjustment, but will be left with their same, old, severely "modified" life expectancy with its high offset deductions. This is how the SSA discriminates against older retirees.

Offsets Forever

If your "*modified*" life expectancy is 11.74 years, then your lump sum should be fully depleted in 11.74 years. However, at the end of the first 11.74 year stretch, the SSA starts a new round for another 11.74 years. After this period ends, the SSA begins again for a third time, deducting the full amount of the lump sum each time.

> For every **$1** you received
> in a government pension,
> the SS will eventually take
> up to **$3** in SS offset deductions.

The SSA uses the outrageous argument that you will save and invest your lump sum at a fixed interest rate of 6% (2005 SS assigned rate). The SSA calculates your offsets on the false assumption that your lump sum is never depleted; is never reduced by withdrawals; is always fully invested; and will earn 6% until you die.

Where is it possible to earn 6% today?

Although interest rates vary yearly, your rate is fixed forever on the day that you applied for SS benefits. The interest rate on the ten-year treasury bond, used as a benchmark by financial firms, changes daily. Why isn't your lump-sum interest rate linked to this benchmark ten-year treasury bond so your interest rate, also, is changed daily or yearly?

The SSA is Double Dipping

The real greedy "double-dipper" is the SSA. The SSA is legally taking from you, your earned SS benefits. The unchallenged fake *"modification"* of your life expectancy by the SSA is unfair to retirees, who worked for years to earn the benefits, that the SSA is now refusing to pay.

**How is your government pension helping you?
It isn't! It will cost you up to
three times more, in offsets, than
the lump sum you actually received.**

The offsets should stop once the offset penalties equal your lump-sum pension. Why should the SSA be allowed to take more than you actually received? Also, why isn't the SSA using a depletion schedule, similar to a home mortgage, to show the actual balance remaining in your lump sum account after each offset deduction?

The SS Trust Fund

The SSA's Trust Fund money was, in 2012, invested in "special issue" treasury bonds at a skimpy 1.37% annual return. Nevertheless, the SSA expects those who retired in 2005, to work magic and continue to receive a fixed 6% annual rate for as long as they live. Is the SSA dreaming?

www.ssa.gov/oact/tr/2013

Let us stop here for a minute and get real. While working, perhaps you invested in an IRA, ROTH, SEP or a 401(k). When you reach 70½ years of age, you will be required to withdraw a minimum amount of money every year from your retirement accounts.

Retirees are no longer saving for retirement because they are retired! If no longer working, contributing money to a ROTH, an IRA or 401(k) is not allowed. You must be working in your own business or be employed in a job in which you will receive a yearly W2 wage statement. Non-working retirees are in the withdrawal and spending phase of their lives. After all, wasn't that the purpose of their retirement investments?

The SSA is not on the same page as retirees. Most are not receiving the SSA's imaginary 6% fixed rate but are likely receiving from 1% to 2%. This low interest rate will not even begin to pay the retirees' increasing expenses. At this point, the retiree may be rapidly depleting his or her lump sum pension to pay for daily living expenses.

> After withdrawals, the lump sum balance becomes
> smaller. Therefore, the shrinking balance will
> earn less and less interest each year.
> Your offsets, however, will be calculated on
> the full original lump sum.
> Does anyone think this practice is fair to retirees?

The end result of these poorly written POMS regulations is to give the commissioner the opportunity to interpret the regulations in any manner, he or she deems appropriate.

Although, you may look, you will not find a single POMS WEP or GPO offset brochure at your local SS office. The lack of information leaves you in the dark and unaware of the regulations. This makes it impossible for you to evaluate the offset calculations used to determine your offset penalties.

> You have been led to believe for years that your SS
> benefit statements were at least somewhat close to what
> you would actually receive.   Sorry, you were deceived!
> Your benefit statements, like the Indian treaties of old, are
> not worth the paper upon which they are written.

In the meantime, the SSA is returning millions of offset penalty dollars back to the SSA Trust Fund every month. Some of these dollars are yours! This offset thievery highlights why offset penalties must be repealed.

secure.ssa.gov/apps10/poms.nsf/lnx/0300605000

The Matching Funds Trick

Are you aware that the "*matching*" funds on your lump sum payout triggered your offset penalties? In some states, you may have the opportunity to refuse the "match." Thereby never paying one cent in WEP or GPO offset penalties. It seems odd that the double-dipping "*windfall*" suddenly disappears if you are allowed to refuse the "*matching*" funds.

In 2017, the SSA however, caught this loophole. Now the SSA now requires that your government pension must NOT be your primary retirement plan and that you must also refuse to take the matching funds.

The word, "*match*," is incorrectly used in place of the correct term "capital gains." A "*match*" indicates that your employer is contributing a fixed dollar sum or percentage each year to your retirement fund to *match* the amount that you contribute.

The pension-paying agency, however, claims they are giving you a match on your withdrawals not on your contributions! ! ! Really?? What kind of nonsense is that? The pension agency is not a corporation; it does not sell, produce, or manufacture anything. The agency does not create profits. The only money it receives is from state government employee contributions plus the interest, dividends and capital gains earned on the pension investments purchased with your pension contributions.

Therefore, the "match" is your own money coming back to you as your original contributions and your share of the investment's earnings.

Any accountant could explain that the increased value derived from the invested contributions are "capital gains!"

It's time for the agency officials to protect the workers who are paying their salaries. The agency should calculate how long a sum will last given a set monthly withdrawal amount and using the benchmark interest rate on the 10-year treasury bill. State agencies should be required to provide the "time specific period" on all lump sum payouts.

The Privileged Few

In 2008, Congress gave selected groups special treatment. The Military Reservists, and The Defense, Finance, and Accounting Service retirees will no longer have WEP offsets because of a special custom-tailored law passed just for them by Congress. They received this offset exemption because they served or are serving our country   *web search public law **108-375 April 2008***

However, teachers, fire and police departments and many others are also serving our country. Why are they not receiving an exemption? Discrimination occurs when one group of government workers is given special treatment while the rest of us must pay offsets.

This special law is outright discrimination.
RS 00605.362 and RS 00605.383

"Generally, your Social Security benefits as a spouse, widow or widower will NOT be reduced if you are receiving a government pension that is NOT based on your earnings."

The SSA Publication No. 05-10007

As a spouse, if you NEVER worked in a government position, you have the good fortune of being exempt from all offsets. You are in a sweet spot. You will receive 100%

of your Social Security benefits and 100% of your deceased spouse's government pension if you were his or her designated beneficiary.

Although, your deceased spouse was required to pay a WEP penalty, you, as his or her surviving spouse, will not. Upon the death of your spouse, you will receive 100% of both pensions without any WEP penalties. Common sense tells us that this is not right.

The person, who earned the pensions, was not allowed to collect 100% of his or her own SS and government pensions. However, his or her spouse, who neither worked, nor paid FICA taxes, will collect 100% of both. The surviving spouse will also receive the $255 death benefit. These WEP policies are illogical and unfair.

Equalization is Not Working

The rationale behind the WEP offset regulations is based upon the false belief that all government retirees receive a huge government pension therefore, the offsets are not causing a hardship. The reality is that a few, top-level, government retirees will receive a large pension. However, only *one in five* will qualify for a pension of 50% or more of their highest three-year average yearly wage.

The typical government employee, with 16 years of service, receives about 15% of his or her highest three-year average wage. By paying smaller pensions to workers with short-term careers, the state pension agencies use the short-term workers' contributions to subsidize the larger pensions paid to the long-term state employees.

However, as distorted as this picture is, it only tells half of the story. The majority of short-term state government workers do not receive a pension. Therefore, they are NOT included in the statistics.   **Hrept. 105-842/ Serial 105-49**

WEP severely hurts the low-wage, short-term employees, who may have worked split shifts, nights, holidays, and weekends. Some of these employees are the school lunch workers, janitors, and bus drivers who do not retire with a large government pension.

The work of police and fire department personnel is often dangerous and even deadly.

WEP was never intended to be applied to low-income or short-term workers.

The WEP offsets, meant to equalize all retirees, have had the opposite effect by lowering many government retirees' total income from their two pensions to less than that of their peers on SS alone.

In 2015, the average WEP offset was $520 per month, leaving the average government retiree with $816 in SS benefits vs those on Social Security alone who on average received $1,336 per month.   ssa.gov/policy/docs/OIG 9-09-2015
                                      and   AEI Economic Perspectives 3/ 2014 Andrew G. Biggs

Many public retirees receive a small pension of only a few hundred dollars and need food stamps, housing assistance and other welfare handouts to replace the benefits lost to offset penalties. Women make up 98% of these retirees.

Do you think women are asking too much when they ask not to be punished in retirement with these harsh offset penalties?   crs.gov 98-35 06/30/2015 by Gary Sidor

Congress

The WEP "equalization" has intensified the daily struggle of retirees living in or near poverty. If unable to maintain their home, many retirees are forced to sell or apply for a reverse mortgage. Reverse mortgages, now popular, are a quick source of income which only temporarily postpones their poverty. In 2013, 48 million people were receiving food stamps. Retirement is once again becoming something to fear, especially if you are a woman.

We can look back to 1983 and President Reagan for this fiasco. The offset regulations, which seemed logical at the time, have become a nightmare for millions of government retirees, costing them thousands of dollars every year.

Congress needs to review the POMS regulations, especially the fake *Lifetime Table in POMS RS 00605.364,* which artificially reduces a retiree's life expectancy. Congress must stop penalizing workers who split their careers between public service and SS covered work.

See Appendix E, page 240, for the full version of: POMS RS 00605.364

We know Congress and the SSA can move rapidly to change existing regulations, if they so choose. Just look how quickly they closed the loophole on the "file-and-suspend" strategy.

**Congress could move
just as quickly
to repeal WEP, GPO and the
DE offsets.**

To learn what the former
"file-and-suspend" strategy
was all about,
read the book,

Get What's Yours

by: Lawrence Kotlikoff

www.getwhatsyours.org

Chapter 6

Government Pension Offset

$\mathcal{T}$he **Government Pension Offset, GPO,** applies to you if you are claiming SS benefits, as a surviving or divorced spouse, *upon a retired or deceased partner*, and if you will be or are receiving a government pension based upon *your own* civil service employment. The purpose of the GPO is to reduce your SS spousal benefits *if you are NOT financially dependent* upon your spouse or ex-spouse.

Your GPO penalty will be two-thirds of your monthly government pension deducted from your monthly surviving spousal SS benefits. Out of ten spousal applications, nine will have their spousal benefits completely wiped out by the GPO penalty. Your GPO offset is calculated by the SSA, who uses the formula found in POMS GN 608.100. A full version of this regulation may be found on the following web site: **ssa.gov/poms.../0202608100**

Who is " NOT Dependent?"

Many spouses believe they will be entitled to collect 100% of their spouse's SS benefits after their spouse dies. No matter how small the surviving spouses income, if the surviving spouse earned any FICA taxable income or will receive any income from a government pension, the SSA considers them *NOT financially dependent.*

What is earned income?

Earned income includes wages or net earnings from employment and any pensions where you did NOT pay FICA SS taxes, such as a state pension.

crosslandgroup.net/_uploads/faqsocialsecurityretirementbenefits.pdf

During your marriage, your spouse may have provided the majority of your household's income, while you may have sacrificed your career to help your spouse climb the corporate ladder. The fact that you are unable to support yourself on your own pension income is NEVER taken into consideration when the SS calculates your GPO penalty. No minimum level of earned income for GPO calculations has been established to determine when one is truly "dependent" upon his or her spouse. Your GPO offset penalty could take 100% of your spousal SS benefits.

Why is the GPO penalty not limited to 50%
of your SS benefits like WEP?

And, why isn't there a low-income exemption?

Who is Dependent?

Social Security does not count unearned income from interest, dividends, rental income, stocks, bonds, real estate investments, 401k(s), insurance policies, annuities, inheritances, IRA's or a private pension. However, your state government pension is the one exception, it will be counted as earned income.

Although a retiree may be very wealthy, or receive a large monthly income from unearned income, the SSA classifies them as *dependent*. Therefore, they will NOT PAY a GPO offset penalty.

However, the former-working-now-struggling-to-survive spouse, is classified as *independent* because he or she earned taxable money, no matter how little. Therefore, the surviving spouse must pay a GPO penalty every month for the rest of his or her life.   finance.zacks.com 401(k)s & IRAs

The Working Class vs The Idle Rich

Money is money. Income is income. What difference should it make how it is acquired? Why should you be treated differently because you "worked" and "earned" your money?

> **If your spouse or ex-spouse paid FICA taxes you should receive 100% of your spousal benefits, if you are eligible, .**

Both the idle rich along with street panhandlers, who do not work but receive their unearned income from handouts, are classified as "*dependents*." Each will receive 100% of his or her spousal benefits without GPO penalties.

This policy is backward.

What's "W'ong" With This Picture?

However, the *independent* surviving or ex-spouse, <u>who worked</u>, will have the maximum GPO penalty applied to any benefits claimed on the SS earnings record of his or her or deceased spouse.

For example, if the surviving spouse has his or her own government pension of $2,100, then two-thirds of this, or $1,400, will be the monthly SS GPO deduction. If his or her deceased spouse or ex was receiving a SS benefit of $1,600 per month the $1,400 GPO deduction reduces the surviving spousal SS benefit to only $200. Ironically, the spouse who <u>NEVER</u> *worked*, will receive both:

1. *The full $1,600 surviving spousal SS benefit without a penalty.*
2. *The deceased spouse's government pension of $2,100, without a GPO offset. (if they are the beneficiary)*
3. *For a total of $3,700*

The Government Pension Offset states:

> *"Your Social Security benefits as a spouse,*
> *widow, or widower will NOT be reduced*
> *if you are receiving a government pension*
> *that is __NOT__ based on your earnings."*
>
> SSA Publication #05-10007

GPO was meant to "equalize" the working spouse who receives a government pension. Unfortunately, the GPO penalty is not working as intended. In fact it reduces a state government worker's SS benefits to less than that of the spouse who never worked or worked in only SS covered jobs.

So let's review this phenomenon again. The spouse who worked and earned a state government pension will pay the maximum GPO offset penalty if receiving SS benefits as a surviving spouse. In our example, the spouse will receive only a $200 survivors' SS benefit plus his or her own $2,100 government pension, for a total of $2,300.

However, the non-working surviving spouse, is entitled to the full $1,600 SS benefit of the deceased spouse, and the full $2,100 of the deceased spouses' state pension without a GPO penalty for a total of $3,700.

While the spouse who worked receives $2,300, the spouse who NEVER worked receives $3,700, or $1,400 more.

This picture is out of focus; does not make sense, and punishes working spouses.   However, this picture emphasis the inequality that the "equalization" has caused from the unfair and poorly written offset regulations.

The surviving spouse, if married to the deceased when they died, will receive a $255 death benefit as well. Today's funeral costs average $10,000. Therefore, the $255 SS death benefit is not enough, and it falls quite short of the cost of buying the poor stiff a coffin.

The Losers Club

The GPO penalty is most punishing to the poor, mainly women retirees, who can least afford the income loss. Of the 6.5 million retirees affected by GPO, 81% are women. Survivors receive on average a $1,311 SS benefit before the GPO offset penalty is deducted.

ssa.gov/policy/docs/quickfacts/stat_snapshot/ Nov.2017

In 2013, 615,000 survivors had their spousal benefits reduced by the GPO. This figure does not include those who felt it was useless to file. On average, women received a civil service pension of $1,977 with a $821 GPO penalty while the average man received $3,063 with only a $460 GPO penalty. www.crs.gov RL-32453 4/23/12 Gary Sidor

On average, women will receive $1,200 less per month as compared to men and pay offsets equaling $34 per $100 of their income. Men pay only $15 per $100. In 2015, women were paid 80% of the wages paid to men for equal work. For middle-skilled occupations, a women received only 66% of a man's wages. Women were also unlikely to qualify for the 30-year substantial earnings exemption.

iwpr.org/issue/pay-equity-discrimination 4/26/2017

Among those placed in the "*struggling*" category, which means that an individual had both short-and long-term financial worries, Willis Towers Watson says that women outpaced men.

If you are a woman, your chances of living in poverty when you pass 65 are 80% higher than for a man. In 2015, 24 million women lived in poverty. Today, many women fear that a major financial crisis could plunge them into bankruptcy. talkpoverty.org/basics/ 2015

Life Expectancy Confusion

A woman or man, at age 55 after June, 2016, has four different life expectancies (LE) each one *calculated by the SSA.* The four LE's range from a high of 30.8 years to a low of 13.26 years.

Remember the lump sum is divided by your LE. The smaller your LE number is, the larger your monthly offset deduction will be.

The Four Age 55 SS LE Variations:

SS: Real LE   30.8 years
www.ssa.gov/planners/lifeexpectancy.html
SSA Life Expectancy Calculator.

SS Actuarial Study   28.15 years
www.ssa.gov/oact/NOTES/s2000s.html
Table 6 2020 & Study No. 120

SS: WEP Table (fake)   18.06 years
POMS RS 00605.364
ssa.gov/poms../00605.364

SS: GPO Table (fake)   13.26 years
POMS GN 02608.400
ssa.gov/poms.nsf/lnx/0202608400

By using the lowest fake LE of 13.26 years to calculate the GPO offset penalty amount, the SS has been able to double the monthly offset deduction for anyone age 55 on or before June, 2007.

The SSA, using the fake modified Lifetime Tables, in both the WEP and GPO regulations, will deny you all or part of your SS benefits.

If you can't figure out what's going on with your LE, join the crowd. Your LE is an SS crapshoot played with loaded dice and the SS always seems to win.

Another regulation, from the *Office of the Inspector General*, adds even more confusion. It reads as follows:

> *"...SSA considers the beneficiary's life expectancy and age at the time of the award to prorate the lump sum payment into a monthly GPO amount."*

This statement clearly says that the SSA is to use your "life expectancy." It does not mention that your real LE would be cut in half (faked & modified) by the SSA.

oig.ssa.gov/.../A-09-13-23049.pdf   see article:
"Incorrect Use of Lump sum Pension Amounts"

Due to the poorly written GPO regulations, the SS Commissioner and the SS attorneys are able to easily interpret the meaning of these regulations to favor the SSA.

Why are words "life expectancy" not written
in the WEP and GPO tables,
rather than the word "lifetime?"

The SS Commissioner should be brought before Congress to answer why the SSA deliberately "fakes" our life expectancy to double and even triple our monthly offset deductions. The SS is using these "fake modifications" to fleece us of our earned SS pension dollars.

The WEP and GPO "fake modifications"
to our life expectancies need to stop.

Floundering In The Dark

The SSA simplifies the seriousness of the offsets by using the excuse that everyone had ample time, since 1983, to change his or her retirement plans. However, workers were neither aware of, nor heard about "offset" penalties until officially "notified" in 2005. The amount of time, considered "ample," has never been defined.

Not until January of 2005, did the SSA require that public state, city, and local employers who had a private pension plan give the *SSA-1945* "notification" to their employees. This notification explains how the offset penalties would affect their SS benefits. To this day, the SSA has never offered an explanation as   to why   the mandatory "notification" requirement was delayed   for 21-years.
www.ssa.gov/forms/ssa-1945.pdf

Even if a government worker immediately quit his or her civil service job, he or she would not avoid the offset penalties which are forever linked to their government job.

How a worker was to change his or her retirement plans has never been explained. Just what "changes" does the SSA mean? If you work in a state with a public pension plan, were you expected to uproot your family and move to a state where you would not face offsets?

Maybe you were expected to forget about a career as a teacher, fire fighter, or police officer in any state that would eventually entangle you in offset penalties.

On the other hand, if unable to opt out of your present position, were you expected to sacrifice a greater-than-average portion of your current income to invest in stocks, real estate, or other investments with the hope of replacing your lost SS benefits?

The SSA leaves workers on their own to flounder in the dark without knowing which course they should take. Workers know that the current offset regulations could be rewritten just as suddenly as the "file and suspend" strategy. The newly rewritten file and suspend regulations gave eligible spouses only six months to take advantage of the option before it ended on April 30, 2016. I guess six months is what the SSA considers "ample" time.

How quickly the SSA can rewrite a POMS regulation when they want to!

It is possible, that a worker who makes changes to his or her retirement plans today, could find in a few years, that a newly rewritten offset regulation would, once again, alter, and unwind his or her new retirement plans.

Judge Olson

SSA's Judge Olson, in his decision, wrote that the WEP and GPO "*Modified Lifetime Tables*" are in fact the "lifetime" of a lump sum, similar to a payment schedule for a house mortgage, and should not be confused with a person's life expectancy, as they are not one and the same.

The offset deductions, Judge Olson wrote, "*do have an ending date*" which occurs when all the 140.9 months of deductions have been paid. However, this short-lived decision was quickly overturned by the Commissioner.

The SS Commissioner reversed Judge Olson's meticulously and carefully thought out decision by claiming that the *"offsets never end "* and Judge Olson made an "error in law." Who is wrong, Judge Olson or the Commissioner? More about Judge Olson on p. 197.

When your lump sum pension shows a zero balance, you are no longer considered to be receiving a government pension. Since you no longer have a government pension you should not have any further SS offset deductions. The following SS regulation would become effective.

".. if the pension ceases and the NH (SS number holder) is no longer entitled to the pension, recompute the PIA, primary insurance account, without considering the pension effective with the first month for which the claimant is no longer entitled to the pension"

ALJ Lyle Olson from *POMS RS605.364 D*

It sounds great! However, I have not heard of a single person who has had his or her SS benefits fully restored and their offsets discontinued. This regulation appears to be *USELESS*. SSA /Wicks Appeal CO 9/6/11

No Adjustments

Your lump sum amount, after 12 months of payments, should be recalculated and your offset penalty adjusted on a yearly basis similar to the way the SS calculates your yearly COLA.

Each year, your lump sum amount becomes smaller and will eventually reach a zero balance. At this point, the pension is gone and your GPO or WEP offset deductions from your SS checks should stop, However, this never happens.

For the rest of your life, the SSA will calculate your monthly offset amount upon the full, original, lump sum amount.

It does not matter one iota to the SSA that your lump sum slowly depletes overtime. However, the SSA goes on, year in and year out, assuming the full 100% of your lump sum is invested and earning a high fixed rate of interest permanently set by the SSA on the day you applied for your SS benefits.

Trust Fund Shortfall Blame Game

The SS Trustees helped to create the Trust Fund shortfall by buying "special issue" bonds from the U.S. Currently, the SS Trust Fund has almost three trillion dollars invested in these underperforming low interest rate bonds. Many now have negative returns.

This means our SS FICA taxes, which are funneled into these "specially issued," low-interest bonds, are losing money. The SSA points fingers at others for the pending shortages in the fund, rather than looking at its own financial ineptness.

Trustees Annual Report SS Trust Funds 6/2012
U.S. Government Publishing Office, p. 37 Also see Chapter 8.

The SSA should stop operating under the outdated 1935 formulas and old policies, written during a time when few women worked. Today, we live in a world where most women work and many never marry their partners. The 1983 offset regulations punish these women.

The SSA independent regulatory agency is run like a dictatorship, and its justice system is a joke. It is working for the SSA, but not for retirees and certainly not women! These POMS regulations are constantly being challenged in one court after another. If highly qualified, experienced, SS judges, like Judge Olson, are having their decisions overturned repeatedly by the Commissioner, why have a SSA justice system?

Our civil service retirees deserve better.

Steve Goss,

Chief Actuary at the Social Security Admin.

You may ask him anything using:

twitter.com/SocialSecuriy/status/49635 39341 69354 240

or
www.reddit.com/r/IAmA/comments/2clv3c/
I-am-steve-goss

Chapter 7

Dual Entitlement Rule

𝕸illions of retirees who have been married 10 years or more will be severely penalized by the 1939 Dual Entitlement Rule, DE. Covering all 50 states, this 70-year old rule could also apply to you, if you have been or were married for 10 years or more, even if you are now divorced or widowed. Of the three offsets, WEP, GPO, and DE, the DE Rule is the most costly and affects the greatest number of retirees.

The DE regulation requires that 100% of your own Social Security benefits be subtracted from any SS spousal benefits you are eligible to receive.

The latest number shows 6.4 million women, 98%, and 200,000 thousand men, 2%, are penalized by the DE rule. The DE offset will cost these retirees over *100 billion dollars in one year alone.*

Dual Entitlement

When filing for Social Security you may be entitled to two SS benefits based upon:

1. Your own SS earnings account, or
2. Your spouse, or an Ex's SS earnings account.

The SS claim will be based upon the account, which will give you the largest SS benefit or the account you prefer they use. Many retirees think that the SSA substitutes one spousal benefit entirely for the other, as in an either/or exchange, but this is not the case.

If one married spouse plans to claim SS benefits on the earnings of the other spouse, they will receive only the amount over and above their own SS benefit.

The larger SS, Primary Insurance Account, PIA,

will be offset by the amount of the

smaller SS account dollar for dollar.

Example of How Your Dual Entitlement
Offset is Applied:

If both spouses are alive, the first spouse with the smaller $800 SS benefit is eligible to receive 50% of the second spouse's $2,400 SS benefit, or $1,200.

The DE penalty however, will deduct the equivalent amount of $800 from the $1,200, leaving the first spouse with his or her own $800 and only the additional spousal benefit of $400.

Formula: The living spouse's $1,200 minus your $800 gives you an additional $400 added to your $800.

However, if the second spouse is deceased, the surviving spouse would receive his or her own SS pension of $800 plus an additional $1,600 from the deceased spouse's $2,400 pension.

Formula: Deceased spouse's $2,400 minus your $800 gives you an additional $1,600. Your $800 and the $1,600 equal $2,400.

In both fictional scenarios, the spouse loses $800 due to the DE penalty.

If DE was to be repealed, the formulas would be

$800 + $1,200 for $2,400 if your spouse is alive or

$800 + $2,400 for $3,400 if your spouse is decease.

RS 00615.020   and   socialsecuritybenefitshandbook.com, section 602

The Dual Entitlement offset is especially harsh on surviving women who make up the largest group and lose 34% of their SS benefits to offset deductions.

When a woman files for spousal benefits, the SSA withholds, on average, a $580 DE offset penalty from her spousal benefit. This offset is deducted each and every month for the rest of her life.   www.crs.gov RL32453

When told how much their spousal SS benefit would be after the DE deduction, many retirees are silent and accept the offset penalty without complaining. Very few of the spouses affected file an appeal or object to this life-changing DE offset. This unchallenged DE rule causes millions of retirees to lose thousands of their spousal benefit dollars every year.   rs.gov RL32453 2/10/2011

If you, as a surviving spouse, are receiving both a SS pension and a government pension based upon your own work, you will have a second offset deduction, the GPO in addition to your DE offset.

Very few retirees escape these offsets, while the wealthier retired workers, with private investments and individual retirement accounts, usually pay the smallest penalties or none at all.

Before 1983

Before 1983, each spouse had the right to collect his or her own SS benefits and the right to receive 50% of the living spouse's SS benefits or the full 100% if the spouse was deceased. Dual Entitlement put a stop to this strategy. *The working spouse receives the same SS benefits as the spouse who never worked!*

ssa.gov.planners/retire/gro.html

I know what you are thinking! Why should the married spouse be able to collect two pensions? How would you feel if these were separate checking accounts and our government required both working spouses to make monthly deposits? Then upon retirement, the government would tell the spouse with the smaller checking account balance that he or she would never receive the money in his or her account. Instead, the SS would take all the money in the account and deposit every dollar back into the SS Trust Fund.

This is how Dual Entitlement works: both spouses work, and both pay for SS retirement insurance, but cannot collect benefits on both accounts when one spouse dies.

Let us look at another scenario. Let us say you both own your own car. You both pay your own insurance premiums. Then one day your garage burns down and both cars are destroyed. What would you say if the insurance company said that only one car could qualify for a compensation check?   The owner of the second car, who paid for insurance also, would receive nothing.

**Would you just passively accept this
decision without complaining?**

**Of course you wouldn't, nor should you accept,
without complaining, the DE offset penalty.**

Of course, if both spouses are alive, collecting on which ever account gives you the largest SS benefit, is usually your best choice. However, it is when one spouse dies that the GPO and DE offset penalties will decimate the surviving spouse.

If your second pension was NOT a SS pension, there would be no offset penalties. The surviving spouse would be eligible to receive both SS and the private 401(k), IRA, Roth or other similar personal investment pension.

**Why should the spouse, who never worked
and never paid one cent in FICA taxes,
be able to collect 100% of his or
her deceased spouse's SS?**

In contrast, the spouse who worked will receive only the amount over and above his or her own SS benefit.

The working spouse has been "equalized!"
he or she will receive NOTHING EXTRA
from the FICA taxes paid.

The American belief that you "get what you pay for, nothing more; nothing less is, when one applies for SS, untrue. Under the SS DE offset regulations, you get *nothing more.*

WHY should a married spouse work,
when the spouse who worked and
the spouse who never worked
receive the same SS benefits?

Work is for Idiots

The SSA has the wrong incentives regarding spouses who work. The working spouses are victimized by the SSA, who punishes them with Dual Entitlement, DE, offsets.

Why put up with the hassles and demands of work when the non-working spouse will receive the same SS benefits as the spouse who worked? The working spouse should be rewarded, not punished, by receiving 100% of both his or her own earned SS pension plus spousal benefits.

If the offset regulations are not going to be repealed, then the SSA should consider giving the working spouse

1. a reduced offset penalty;

2. offer credits toward offsets; or

3. a refund of the FICA taxes paid.

Expenses

When your spouse dies, your household expenses will be nearly the same for heat, water, property taxes, air conditioning, house repairs, seasonal lawn upkeep, leaf removal, and perhaps, the plowing and shoveling of snow. If you cannot do these chores yourself, you face the additional cost of hiring others to help. A one-person household could even have higher expenses than when he or she had a spouse.

Your vehicle maintenance and its insurance expense, your home owner's insurance; the cost to replace an appliance; repair or replace a hot water heater, a furnace, or a leaky roof will not change. As the surviving spouse, you may have to pay all the funeral bills out of your own pocket. In addition, if no longer allowed to drive, you may have the additional expense of public transportation.

As their medical expenses increase, many retirees resort to either cutting their pills in half or skipping several days to make their prescriptions last longer. Many retirees put off visiting their doctor when sick, waiting until their health deteriorates so badly that they end up in the emergency room or are admitted to the hospital.

The single retiree, trying to live on a severely reduced income, will also change food choices by substituting cheaper, less healthy items. These substitutions are usually higher in starch and lower in nutritional value. High quality proteins, like meat, chicken, and fish, are some of the first items reduced or eliminated. Over time this poor nutritional diet may accelerate declining health.

If a retiree owns a home, the day may arrive when the GPO and/or DE penalty of $800 may mean that the surviving spouse cannot afford the help required to stay and live in the home.

House repairs may be postponed or never done at all, as the surviving spouse struggles on with a "make do" determination. Many spouses will eventually sell, downsize, or live with a relative. In some cases, the widow or widower is moved directly into a nursing home.

The Great Migration

In desperation, if a retiree is unable to buy food, pay for prescriptions, pay an electric bill, or turned the heat down any lower, the retiree begins to migrate to other welfare programs.

The migrating retiree begins by requesting help from government agencies and the welfare office. Most begin by applying for food stamps, rental assistance, heating funds, Medicaid, and free food from their local food bank.

The retirees' expenses migrate with them. This migration will cost the government more in the long run than if the offsets were simply repealed.

Neither the retiree

nor his or her

living expenses disappear!

.

The SS **COST** to support retired
workers does not go away

it Migrates

The SSA, using offset penalties, takes the retiree's *unpaid SS benefit money* and returns it to the SS Trust Fund. This shortsighted strategy reduces the SS benefit payments from the Trust Fund but shifts the retiree's expenses to other government programs.

**A study has also shown that 15%
of money-strapped seniors
will resort to shoplifting.**

www.thisamericanlife.org/radio-archives/episode/135/llure-of-crime

Saving money by withholding benefits from retirees is an ineffective strategy in the long run. It seems that the SSA neither does not look at, nor want to see, the big picture. Although, offsets are costly to repeal, emergency room visits, hospital stays, nursing homes, and providing welfare services are more expensive.

**These former workers
earned their SS benefits.**

Why are these retirees so heartlessly abused by Congress and the SSA, who is withholding the SS benefits that these civil service workers, earned, paid for, and are entitled to collect, like other SS beneficiaries?

**Offsets show the dreadfully cruel,
abusive way in which our government
treats civil servant retirees.**

Social Security - No Guarantees

The SSA could provide better options for survivors by giving them a greater death benefit. For example, when a person dies, the SS could continue to pay, the deceased *FULL* SS benefit check to a surviving spouse, without GPO penalties, for several years. This would give the spouse time to adjust to a life style with far less income.

This option would insure your survivors were not left to struggle as the deceased SS benefit check, after GPO penalties is suddenly reduced or stops altogether.

The SS, should increase the death benefit to $10,000. Given the stressful death of one's spouse, an increase in the death benefit would mean the funeral costs could easily be paid without the possibility of the survivor(s) going into debt, or filing for bankruptcy.

If your other pension or pensions are from a retirement plan such as a 401(k), SEP, ROTH or Traditional IRA, the SS does not apply offset penalties. However, the SSA is aggressive in penalizing retirees with offsets when their second pension is from another SS account.

Your having two SS pensions does not justify the SSA's position that an offset penalty has to be paid. The poorest retirees, who rely on the second SS pension, lose either half or all of this pension because they pay the largest percentage of their SS income in offset penalties.

If other SS retirement options were available, part of your FICA taxes could be invested in a private, offset penalty-free retirement account, instead of the current one-and-only SS plan with its skimpy pension benefits.

How can a state retirement plan, with higher administration costs, pay larger benefits?

In the meantime, the SSA, with little overhead, is claiming that it is facing the possibility of a shortage.

Annuities – A "Time Certain" Guarantee

An annuity is an insurance policy purchased with a single lump sum or with payments prior to or after retirement. Our SS benefits are also an annuity. The commercial annuity policy, however, has a very unique and important option.

The "time certain" option is a guarantee that once you begin taking payments, and should you die within the "time certain" period, your beneficiaries will receive your remaining payments.

You choose the length of time for the "time certain" period which is usually somewhere between five to twenty years. However, the longer the length of time chosen, the smaller each payment will be for you and your beneficiaries.

Many a retiree believes that the original annuity investment will be inherited by the family or the beneficiaries. They are shocked to learn that once they draw their first payment, called annuitizing, all of

the money invested in the annuity belongs either to the insurance company or the entity that issued the annuity policy.

Should you die within the "time certain," your family or beneficiaries will receive only the *remaining payments* in the "time certain" period.

However, you as the owner of the annuity, even if the "time certain" period has passed, will continue to receive annuity payments for the rest of your life.

Other Retirement Plans vs Social Security

Although our government encourages workers to save for retirement, for 86 million workers, whose average yearly wage in 2016 was $31,099 or less, saving is nearly impossible. www.thedailybeast.com/articles/2016/10/21 average wages

In 2018 only 53% of workers were covered by an employer-sponsored 401(k) or other retirement plan. Those who contribute to a 401(k) plan usually contribute only up to the employers' match and then stop. For 59% of boomers Social Security will become the major source of income in retirement.   income. https://www.fool.com/retirement/2018/02/12

In 2018, workers in SS covered jobs, will pay a 7.65% FICA tax on wages up to $128,400, and their employer pays an equal amount. The combined total is 15.30%. At the $128,400 level the employee and employer combined FICA taxes for 2018 will equal $19,645.20.

A retiree's FICA contributions, managed by the Trustees for the SS Trust Fund, have had returns that average a measly ½ of 1% per year.

CRS 3/2016 #16-4

Private Investment Account Advantages

You own *all the money* in your account.
You choose the amount you will contribute.

You choose the investments.
You may have a ROTH, SEP,
Traditional IRA or a 401(k) plan.

You can choose bonds, stocks, mutual funds or EFT's.
You receive the all interest, dividends, and capital gains.

You never pay an offset penalty.
No WEP - No GPO - No DE.

Personal accounts do not affect your SS benefits.
You do not need 40 quarters to receive your money.

You do not have to participate in these investments.
If you participate, you can stop at any time.

You choose the amount you will withdraw.
You choose how often you will take withdrawals.
You can take emergency withdrawals.

Spouses are immediately eligible upon marriage.
You choose your beneficiary(s), and you
may have more than one.

Beneficiaries do not need to be a family member.
Your beneficiaries have several payout options.

Beneficiaries receive <u>ALL THE MONEY</u> in your account.

Roth IRA disbursements are tax-free.

Social Security Disadvantages

All your contributions belong to the SS Trust Fund.
The SS has only one investment, "special issue" gov't bonds.
Other investment options are NOT available.

You face massive WEP, GPO and DE offset penalties.

You must earn 40 SS quarters (10 years) to be eligible.
There are no refunds if you fall short
of the eligibility requirement.

You are required by law to participate.

You could have two offset penalties.
Your working spouse will NOT receive 100% of your SS pension.

You must be married 10 years to collect spousal benefits.
After the offset penalties, your surviving
spouse may receive nothing.

SS pays a tiny $255 death benefit.
Your monthly benefit payment is set by the SSA.

Retirees with a government pension could lose
all of their SS benefits.

Only your married spouse or child may be your beneficiary.

The only available payout option is the monthly annuity.

SS benefits are taxable if you earn over $25,000.

The Wealthy

The highly paid CEO's, executives, and upper level employees quickly exceed the FICA taxable wage base of $128,400. Once they reach this amount, they will no longer have FICA taxes deducted from their wages. However, there is no wage cap on the 1.45% tax for Medicare and if you make over $200,000 you will be taxed an addition 0.9% Medicare surtax.

These CEO's, executives and upper level employees can then divert the same 7.65% they would have paid in FICA taxes to their own private retirement investments.

In 40 years, (keeping everything constant), the $19,645.20 annual maximum FICA contributions would total a whopping $785,808.

If these contributions were invested monthly in the stock market,which on average earns 8% per year,they would have grown to over five million dollars!

Even the wealthy CEOs, receiving the maximum SS benefit of $2,788 per month in 2018, will only receive a return of ½ of 1% on their FICA contributions.

www.ssa.gov/policy/docs/chartbooks/fast_facts/2017
www.ssa.gov/policy/docs   SSS Pub. No. 13-11785

Al Gore and The " Motherhood" Penalty

Under the current law, a worker's Social Security benefits are based upon his or her average earnings over 35 years. However, because Moms, the likely family caretaker, often take years off from their careers to raise children. The typical Mom has only 27 years with ANY earnings.

Working Moms, in particular, are penalized by the current system, when upon retiring and facing DE offsets, they discover that they will receive no additional benefits from their own work and all the FICA taxes they paid. A mother, if married for ten years or more, will simply draw spousal benefits based on the SS earnings of the husband.

jay.law.ou.edu/faculty/jforman/Opeds/jr8-00(SS-working-mothers).htm

**Al Gore calls this the "motherhood penalty."
To be fair to Moms, Al Gore feels that we should
either raise benefits for Moms who paid FICA
taxes or repeal the Dual Entitlement Rule.**

Social Security

"Divide and conquer" favors the SSA as workers complain about the generous pensions received by civil servants. Instead they should unit to demand that everyone receive the SS benefits they earned.

The SSA neither mentions its lousy returns on their "special issue" treasury bonds, nor reports how many workers never receive a dime in benefits due to their having died before reaching retirement.

The SSA also fails to report the thousands of spouses denied benefits because they fell short of the 10-year marriage requirement nor those not eligible for benefits because they failed to have the required 40 quarters. The FICA taxes paid by these workers is kept by the SSA.

It is not the retiree's fault that we have a financially inefficient and greedy SSA.

The SSA says the that civil service employees did not pay FICA taxes while working in a public position. True, but the SSA fails to explain that the amount of a retiree's SS benefit is based **ONLY** on the earnings from working in a SS covered position.

If you contribute little to SS, you receive little.

SS is NOT welfare.
It is NOT a freebie.
It is EARNED.

Yet, many civil retirees and their spouses are denied all or part of their earned SS benefits.

The SSA, with the blessing of Congress, commits
legalized robbery by denying SS benefits
to qualified retirees.

The Big Messy Offset Maze

All three offset regulations, WEP, GPO, and DE, are one big mess! They are a maze, a quagmire of confusing, contradictory regulations and bad advice from many of the SS representatives. The only purpose of the offset regulations is to prevent government retirees, who are eligible, from collecting their earned SS benefits.

Currently, there does not appear to be an agreement among SS representatives as to how each regulation is to be applied, and who is to be penalized, for how much and for how long. It is quite common for a SS retiree to receive several, conflicting answers to the same question.

If the average person cannot understand the POMS regulations and, why the members of Congress, attorneys, SSA representatives, and the courts are constantly changing each other's decisions, then:

"Houston, we have a problem."

At this time, the SSA aggressively applies offset penalties ONLY to the public workers in the states that force their workers into the state's private pension plan.

> How large or small a government pension one receives should NOT be used to dismiss the SSA's responsibility to pay a person his or her earned SS benefits.

Retirement Benefits for Congress

Benefits for those in Congress are either based fully or in part on their congressional civil service career. As of October 1, 2015, 344 members had retired.

The congressional taxpayer funded and guaranteed private pension value can be up to 80% of the member's final salary. In 2016, congressional pay was $174,000 per year, which, at an 80% pension rate, equates to a

lifelong pension of $139,200 per year.

Under current laws, taxpayers will not fund nor pay SS benefits to retirees if there is a shortage of money in the SS Trust Fund. However, in contrast, Congress made sure that   their   own private pension plan benefits were taxpayer-funded and guaranteed.

Congress, although civil servants, should be
required to be on SS, not a taxpayer
funded, private pension plan.

senate.gov/CRSpubs/ac0d1dd5-7316-4390-87e6-353589586a89.pdf

or investopedia.com/articles/markets/080416 March 2017

Chapter 8

The SS Trust Fund

𝔖he *English Poor Law of 1601* made each state responsible for the welfare of its citizens. This law was based up on the ideas brought over from England by the colonists. The colonists felt that a government's duty was to provide for the welfare of the poor, whom they viewed as highly undesirable characters and treated them badly.

www.ssa.gov/history/briefhistory3.html

Civil War Pensions

With the creation of Civil War pensions in 1776, the first national pension program for soldiers became the beginning of what today is our Social Security system. Based upon social insurance rather than welfare assistance, it was expanded in 1932 by President Roosevelt. Its expansion created a work-related, contributory system in which works would provide for their own future, economic security through taxes paid while employed.

Title One of the Act of 1932 established the SSA Board, comprised of three members appointed by the President. In 1946, this Board was abolished and replaced by a single person, called the Commissioner, who reports directly to the President.   www.ssa.gov/history/briefhistory3.html

Independent Regulatory Agency vs Independent Agency

The Social Security Administration is an "*independent regulatory*" agency. More specifically, the term may be used to describe agencies, that while constitutionally part of the executive branch, are independent of presidential control, usually because the president's power to dismiss the agency head or a member is limited.

Generally, the heads of *independent regulatory* agencies can only be removed for cause, whereas *independent* agencies, like the Environmental Protection Agency are headed by a cabinet member and serve "at the pleasure of the President." Presidents find that the *independent* agencies are more loyal and in lockstep with their wishes and policy objectives. The department heads may be fired and the independent agency regulations changed by an executive order from the President.

wikipedia.org/wiki/Independent_agencies note: Admin.

Executive Order # 12866

"The American people deserve a regulatory
system that works for them,
not against them,
a regulatory system that *protects and improves*
their health, safety, environment, and well-
being and improves the performance of the
economy without imposing unacceptable or
unreasonable costs on society; regulatory
policies that recognize that the private sector
and private markets are the best engine for
economic growth; regulatory approaches that
respect the role of state, local, and tribal
governments; and regulations that are
effective, consistent, sensible, and
understandable."

"We do NOT have such a regulatory system today."

William J. Clinton - September 30, 1993

Executive Order #12866, requires cost-benefit analysis
but does NOT apply to the SSA.

Although SS is part of the Regulatory Agencies

as an independent agency it is EXEMPT

from presidential control and executive orders.

Former President Reagan

In 1983, Reagan signed into law the POMS offset regulations for WEP, GPO, and Dual Entitlement. In the period following these 1983 amendments, the Social Security program has run annual surpluses with revenues exceeding the benefit payments and administrative costs.

In 2016, the Social Security Trust Fund had 3 trillion dollars, with billions being added to this surplus every year. The surpluses are invested, by law, in special issue treasury bonds.   ssa,gov./policy/trust-funds June 2016

Under The Gun

**The President supervises the SS Commissioner
who, must loan the Trust Fund money
ONLY to the U.S. government
with its the purchases of the
special issue treasury bonds
as required by Congress.**

Since the President could demand the commissioner voluntarily resign if he or she does not comply, a serious conflict of interest occurs. How can the commissioner perform effectively with a possible resignation request hanging above his or her head?

SSA Today

The Social Security Administration is headquartered in suburban Baltimore with over 65,000 employees nationwide. Social Security benefits are funded by current workers who pay FICA taxes. In 2017, the federal government spent $945 billion on Social Security benefits, and operating costs. At the same time, it took in $1.238 trillion in FICA taxes which produced another yearly surplus of $293 billion.

https://www.thebalance.com/current-u-s-federal-government-tax-revenue-3305762
By Kimberly Amadeo   February 16, 2018

In 2017, it was estimated that 175 million workers were paying FICA taxes while 43 million retirees, age 65 and over, were receiving Social Security benefits.

www.shrm.org Oct 2016

**Since SS benefits can only be paid if there
is money in the Trust Fund,
SS benefits will be reduced or stopped
if the money runs low.**

**The U.S. government
WILL NOT use taxpayer money
to pay SS retirees their benefits.**

To see a current summary of the Trust Fund income and payouts
along with the current average SS benefits, go to:
www.ssa.gov/policy/trust-funds-summary

If the U.S. Government wants low interest rate loans, in return, it should guarantee financial support or a bailout when the SS has shortfalls and faces benefit reductions.

However, state law requires that, state pension agencies, must pay their retirees their promised benefits. State agencies hire financially trained teams to manage the investments and reduce market risk. This helps to insure the retirees' pensions can be paid.

Unlike the SSA, if the state pension funds run low, state taxpayers *WILL* have to foot the bill and pay state retirees their promised pensions.

The contrast is glaring. Not only do state pensions pay twice the benefits for the identical years of work and earnings as compared to those in SS covered positions, but the state pension is also guaranteed and financially backed by the taxpayers.

markhillman.com state pension benefits 1/26/09   and
ssa.gov/news/press/basicfact.html 10/13/2015

State Pensions vs Social Security

The Colorado State PERA* contributions are invested in a variety of financial instruments. The CO state pension agency, whose success has enabled the agency to be

*PERA = Public Employees Retirement Association

generous with its pension benefits, also guarantees a 2% COLA* increase every year. *COLA = Cost-of-living Adjustment

Retirees on SS do not have a COLA guarantee and did not receive a SS benefit increase in 2016. SS retirees received a COLA increase in 2017 of 0.39% (1/3 of 1%). On average, each SS retiree received an extra $4 per month, enough to buy either one loaf of bread or a gallon of gas, but not both.

SS's Broken Promise

When you work in a SS-covered position, you enter into an agreement with the SSA. The agreement becomes active when you pay FICA taxes on your wages, as required by law.

The SS insurance agreement is broken when the SSA denies you your earned benefits.

Although, you are not eligible for SS benefits, you and your employer(s) will never receive a refund of even one penny of the FICA taxes paid.

The SSA's **Program Operations Manual System, POMS,** and its regulations are difficult to find and have been virtually out of sight for 21 years. Public workers are caught off guard by the offset regulations, which are used by the SS to calculate their monthly offset penalty.

See Appendix E for POMS regulations

Illinois State Pensions

In a pension case filed in Illinois, the Supreme Court upheld a ruling by Sangamon County Circuit Judge, John Belz, who said:

"The state of Illinois made a constitutionally protected promise to its employees concerning their pension benefits.

Under established Illinois law, the state of Illinois cannot break this promise."

Regardless of what other pensions the retiree may be receiving, the Supreme Court requires a state to pay promised benefits to its state retirees. Meanwhile the SS, which is exempt, does not have to pay you and me the SS pensions that we earned, paid for, and been promised.

Why are the laws of our land applicable to state pensions but NOT to our SS benefits?

The Trustees Annual Report

Each year, in July, the Board of Trustees publishes its annual report regarding the SS Trust Fund, which includes its special issue bond purchases. In looking at the June 2012 report, we find that the trustees purchased 273 million dollars in special issue treasury bonds from the U.S. government. These bonds pay a small, pathetic 1.37% annual rate of return.

During the same time period, the Vanguard Index 500 Fund, used by financial analysts as a yardstick for comparison, earned a yearly return of 16%, which is over eleven times more!. Smart investors like Hillary Clinton and Warren Buffet both invest in an Index 500 Fund.

In June 2013, the SS trustees purchased another 253 million dollars of special issue treasury bonds with a 1.75% annual rate of return. In the same year, the Vanguard Index 500 Fund returned over 32%, a full 18 times more!

Going back even further, we find similar, poor returns on the required purchases of special issue treasury bonds, sold to the SS Trust Fund by the U.S. government.

In their reports, the trustees merge the dismally low returns of the past five to six years with the higher earning bonds from past years. Although, the combined bond purchases appear to have a decent return, this does not fool anyone.

Our government is using our SS Trust Fund as its own piggy bank to obtain cheap loans.

The Trustees Annual Report is available on the internet.

The bond investment information is usually on page 37.

Search:
Board of Trustees Annual Report SS Trust Funds June 2012
U.S. Government Publishing Office page 37

Your ½% Rate of Return

The Heritage Foundation found the average single male, born after 1966, could expect to receive an annualized real rate of return of less than ½ of 1% on his lifetime of FICA contributions.

We can compare this ½% yearly return

to the private state pension system,

which averages 8%,

or the Vanguard Index 500 Fund,

which has been averaging 10.84%

every year for forty years.

Heritage Foundation Center for Data Analysis Report #98-01
by William W. Beach and Gareth E. Davis   and   vanguard.com VFINX

SS retirees receive a pension, which is about half of the amount paid to civil servants for similar wages and years worked.

Mike Rosen of the Denver Post said:

"SS is a lousy deal for most of us private-sector slobs."

www.denverpost.com 5-26-2011

We are clearly being short changed on the congressionally required Trust Fund bond investments.

It is a real possibility that if investment policies for the Trust Fund are not changed, a cash shortage will result as yearly benefit payments exceed the yearly FICA tax revenues. By 2034, your monthly Social Security benefit could be cut by 25%. This means you will receive $3 for every $4 you now receive.   cbpp.org/research/social-security/policy-basics-top-ten-facts-

Time For A Change

What seemed like a smart investment plan in 1935 has deteriorated badly over the years. As interest rates climb and the bond returns become negative, these special issue treasury bonds will lose value.

In 2018, as interest rates rise, the SSA will be forced to either hold the bonds until they mature and take a loss or sell immediately, again at a loss. Both options are unappealing. The U.S. Treasury, Congress, and the SSA are in a difficult position. Congress needs to take responsibility and amend the restrictive SS Trust Fund investment policies.

All The Eggs in One Basket

The first thing any investment firm advises its clients to do is to diversify their investments. The second thing it advises is to invest in short term bonds, with less than one-year to maturity, when interest rates are low. The SS Trust Fund appears to violate both of these two basic rules.

However, the trustees must invest according to *Section 201(d) of the Social Security Act*, written and passed by Congress over 80 years ago. This law requires that the SS Trust Funds purchase these below market, low-interest, government created, special issue treasury bonds.

When individuals are advised to invest in equities; state pension agencies are investing in a diverse portfolio, which includes stocks; and when the Vanguard Index 500 Fund's annual returns have repeatedly outperformed the treasury bonds, Congress should allow the SSA to consider buying an Index 500 Fund or the ETF (symbol SPY) 500 Index stock.

The current, brain-numbing, 80 year old bond investment policy is increasing the possibility of a future money shortage in the Trust Fund everyday that the SSA is locked into this archaic and restrictive investment policy.

The SSA should consider hiring financial professionals to manage the Trust Fund investments. The state pension agencies have proven that the stock market produces better returns in the long run than only holding bonds. However, the commissioner does not appear to have an action plan to present to Congress to request that the investment policies be updated.

With nearly three trillion dollars currently invested in special issue treasury bonds, one might think that this large amount would put too much upward pressure on the stock market.

The Security Exchange Commission states, in its *"Strengthening Oversight of Market Stability"* testimony, that the average stock market transaction volume cleared and settled averages about $6.6 trillion a day. This means that if 5% of the SS Trust Funds were invested in the stock market, there would be no impact on stock prices due to the large daily volume of security transactions. **www.sec.gov/News/Testimony**

Outdated Investment Policies

Projections by the *Congressional Research Service*, CRS, indicate that the SS Trust Fund could be exhausted in 2034. The commissioner has a fiduciary responsibility to take action while there is time to alter this dire projection. Congress, the commissioner and the trustees should not sit idly by while the SS system tanks.

The SSA's current, low-interest, bond investments are robbing the SS Trust Fund of the revenue it needs to prevent a future shortage. Laws written decades ago need to be reviewed. A strategic plan should be developed to prevent this catastrophic prediction from occurring.

www.crs.gov 8/05/2015 RL33028

Either Increasing the retirement age; continuing to apply offset penalties; or raising taxes are **NOT** acceptable solutions, as these fall mainly on the already struggling, low wage worker.

Many blue-collar workers have jobs that physically wear down their bodies. By the time they reach 60 years old, many are unable to continue working in their trade. Increasing the retirement age hurts these workers.

.

Most white-collar workers, with less physically demanding jobs, already continue to work long past their full retirement date. Therefore, any increase in the retirement age would not significantly reduce the cash outflows from the Trust Fund. Raising the cap for FICA taxes, from the current $128,400 to $5 million or higher, would be a start in the right direction.

The End of "File and Suspend"

The discontinued, file-and-suspend rule dates back to 2000, when Congress adopted the *Senior Citizens' Freedom to Work Act.* According to financial planner, Michael Kitces, of the Pinnacle Advisory Group, the act was intended to make it easier for people, who were at full retirement age or older, to suspend their benefits and go back to work.

Although the rule did not initially attract much attention, financial planners and retirement experts wrote about this provision in the POMS policies, that would allow married couples to use this strategy to increase their spousal benefits.

A growing number of spouses quickly began filing for SS benefits, then suspending them temporarily, to take advantage of this loophole.

Alarmed, the Social Security Administration and Congress moved rather quickly in 2016 to put a stop to the "File and Suspend" strategy. It is astounding, that not until financial planners suggested using this strategy, did the SS officials, finally, after 16 years, become aware of this loophole.

It is even more amazing just how fast the SS laws were changed when the SSA thought it was being taken advantage of by savvy retirees. Current offset regulations, should and could be changed just as quickly.

http://www.aarp.org/work/social-security/info-2015/congress-ends-file-and-suspend.html plus   The Week Mag 11/20/2015 p.33

Out of Touch

The previous commissioner appeared reluctant to take action toward solving the future Trust Fund shortage. We do not need a figurehead, whose only action is to frighten retirees and young workers, with the possibility of SS shortages and benefit cuts.

The SS needs to hire a professional finance team that has been educated and trained in managing stock investments. We need action now to solve the shortages and to receive a higher rate of return on our Trust Fund contributions.

Only a fool repeatedly does the
same thing and expects to
see different results.

A fresh vision
and someone who will
shake up the SSA are needed.

More studies and useless reports
are the last things we need.

Protecting Social Security

Currently, the SSA tells us about the low overhead and low cost to manage the trust funds. We would rather hear of the trustees' making a greater effort to get us better returns on our FICA tax contributions.

We need larger pensions;

a guaranteed yearly COLA increase;

options in our choice of a beneficiary;

transitional benefits;

a larger death benefit;

and a variety of investment plans.

Warren Buffett: Bonds 'Terrible' In Comparison to Stocks

On May 8, 2017, Warren Buffett bashed treasury bonds. He said that stocks are a much better investment for the long term than treasury bonds.

Warren said,

"Bonds are a terrible choice against stocks."

www.barrons.com/articles
1494258737 by Andrew Bary May 8, 2017

Buffet, with $73 billion, is the

second richest man in the world,

When he gives his opinion

on bonds vs. stocks, it pays to listen.

Congress, the commissioner,

and the trustees need to

take action.

The Trust Fund

investment policies need to be

updated immediately!

Chapter 9

Above The Law

𝔒he social insurance concept is characterized as any form of insurance in which a government is an insurer. Thus, insurance is subject to governmental regulation to protect the consumer's interests.

When the Old-Age, Survivors, and Disability Insurance OASDI, Program was created, "insurance" was included in their titles. The purpose of these insurance programs was to replace income that was lost to a family through the retirement, death, or disability of a worker who had earned protection against these "risks."

The workers and their families would have eligibility for their benefits as an *"EARNED RIGHT."* The level of these insurance benefits was based on the average amount the worker earned in their highest 35 years of SS covered jobs,

128   Social Security Offset Penalties

and the benefits were to be paid without a test of economic
need.   **aspe.hhs.gov/sites/default/files/aspe**

Fiduciary

Fiduciary is the legal term that means to put a customers'
interest first. The SSA, however, when it comes to paying
benefit claims, appears to twist the intended meaning of
the POMS regulations in order to deny a retiree's claim for
benefits.

Congress and the SSA singles out and penalizes civil
servants claiming they are receiving a "windfall" if they have
both a government and SS pension. When a worker's
benefit claim is denied, the SSA should be required to
refund their FICA contributions.

> **The offsets violate SSA fiduciary**
>
> **responsibility to pay everyone**
>
> **his or her rightfully earned pension benefits,**
>
> **but this is**
>
> **NOT how the SSA is operating.**

Instead, the Congress punishes civil servants who split
their working careers between SS covered work and work
in a civil service position.

Entitlement it is NOT -- It is Insurance

By using the word "entitlement," Congress gives you, the public, the impression that these are welfare handouts paid with taxpayer dollars. Nothing could be further from the truth.

Social Security is NOT welfare!
It is NOT an entitlement!
It is a worker's prepaid insurance!

The taxpayers do not
contribute one dime to
the SS Trust Fund.

The Trust fund receives only the FICA taxes paid by current workers. These taxes pay every cent of the SS benefits paid to eligible former workers now retired.   These former workers also paid FICA taxes -- this is how they earned their right to collect a SS retirement, disability or a survivor's benefit.

SSA *Fights* Retirees

If future Trust Fund shortages materialize, one cause may be that our FICA contributions are being spent on maintaining a legal department staffed with expensive teams of attorneys who fight never ending appeals.

130 Social Security Offset Penalties

A SSA lawyer, in 2017, had a salary that averaged $97,000. And that is just the beginning as there are SSA judges, paralegals, office personnel and other legal support staff. The legal staff is paid with our FICA tax money taken from our Trust Fund meant for our benefits. To see the complete list of the SS staff and their salaries go to:

www.indeed.com/cmp/Social-Security-Administration/salaries
www.psjd.org/2016-2017 Federal Legal Employment Guide-

Absolute Power Corrupts Absolutely

The SSA spares no expense, and compromise is not possible when the Commissioner is given absolute (a sense of morality lessen as power increases) power and can overturn unfavorable court decisions.

With an unlimited source of cash from our FICA taxes, the Commissioner has no reason
to be efficient or to consider the possibility that paying the offsets may be cheaper
than paying all the SSA attorneys to constantly fight WEP, GPO, and DE appeals.

A Stacked Deck

Retirees apparently do not have a voice that's being heard in any court of law. Court cases are one-sided with the odds stacked against the retiree who must fight the SSA juggernaut at their own expense.

The stress wears down a complaining retiree who must deal with the many delays and numerous delays and appeals filed by the SSA. These appeals and delays are stressful and may deplete a retiree's limited financial resources. The worn-down retiree is easily defeated. Over time, many retirees will die and lose their case by default.

Some judges seem so intimidated by the SSA that they simply agree with the Commissioner.

> ## "We will not reweigh the evidence or substitute our judgement for the Commissioner's."
>
> **U.S. Court of Appeals for the Tenth Circuit**
> **Case No. 13-1542 Decision**

This is NOT impartial, unbiased justice. Retirees are up against a stacked deck when the courts are reluctant to seriously consider a retiree's evidence. The appeals courts appear to automatically rubber-stamp their approval of the Commissioner's decisions.

A Fool and His Money

The SSA has a fiduciary responsibility to invest our FICA contributions wisely and to ensure the Trust Fund monies are safely earning inflation protected returns -- this the SSA has failed to do.

The Trust Fund is losing millions of dollars in potential revenue because of the laws passed by Congress 80 years ago requiring the SS Trust Fund money be invested in special issue Treasury bonds, (loans), to the U.S. Government at below market interest rates.

The average person would stop buying these bonds if they were losing money, yet the SSA, as mandated by laws from Congress, has to keep pumping our FICA contributions into these special money losing junk bonds. The federal government exploits and plunders the SS Trust Fund and siphons away the surplus money thereby draining the fund dry each year.

These bonds rank near the bottom of retirement investments and are underperformers. In many cases, the bonds when redeemed, will buy far less than the day they were sold to the Fund.

Pirates Plunder

The Trust Fund is not a treasure chest to be looted by the U.S. Government. By selling special issue Treasury bonds to the Trust Fund, the government obtains low-cost money they then squanders it on tax subsidies to profitable corporations, spending on foreign rebuilding projects, and tax write-offs for the wealthy.

It's time the Commissioner became proactive and stopped the federal government from using our Trust Fund money, basically, for FREE.

The SSA mission must be to ensure a financially sound Trust Fund. However, the SSA seems to have lost sight of who they are working for, who's paying their salaries and who's paying their bills -- it's not the U.S. Government – it's you and I.

Subsidies for Corporations

The federal government gave tax subsidies to 288 companies over five years totaling a staggering $364 billion.

Five Companies
Wells Fargo - AT&T, - IBM,

General Electric - and Verizon

enjoyed over $*77 billion* in tax breaks during this period. The federal tax code also provides tax subsidies to companies that make video games, build NASCAR race tracks and make movies.

ctj.org/corporatetaxdodgers/sorrystateofcorptaxes

The fact is that the tax laws allow America's biggest companies to shelter almost half of their U.S. profits to avoid paying taxes while receiving subsides funded with tax money from tax-paying workers.

These large subsidies are going to highly profitable corporations including the cash-laden oil companies and large commercial farms; yet, I have not heard of any bills or proposals by Congress to eliminate this costly practice.

The $104 Billion Afghanistan Bill

The Fiscal Times reported that hundreds of millions of dollars are missing in Afghanistan. Auditors said they only had data for $21 billion of the *$66 billion* it spent rebuilding the country.

> *Of the $57 billion paid to the Afghan forces only $17 billion can be traced.*

John Sopko, Special Inspector General for Afghanistan Reconstruction, revealed that most transactions are nearly impossible to track so there is virtually no way to know what happened to a large chunk of money spent before 2010.

Overall, Sopko stated that the U.S. has poured more than *$104 billion* into Afghanistan since 2002.

thefiscaltimes.com/2015 by Brianna Ehley 4/10/15

The $43 Million Gas Station

If the federal government can waste taxpayer's funds to build a $43 million dollar gas station in Afghanistan then Congress should help Americans by supporting a bill to end the DE, WEP, and the GPO offsets.

US spending $43M on gas station in Afghanistan 11/2/15 FoxNews.com

"Free Stuff" For The Rich

Through loopholes in the tax code, the government gifts wealthy taxpayers, like President Trump, with more than *$900 billion a year*, that's right it's every year, with tax write-offs – more than is spent on welfare programs.

Using the mortgage interest tax deduction, wealthy people receive huge tax breaks on their multi-million dollars homes. In fact, mortgage interest write-offs cost the government three times what it pays out in rental assistance to the poor.

Social Security, especially for us -- the other 99% who do pay taxes -- is our main source of retirement income.

The measure of a country is how well they take care of all their citizens, not just the rich, large corporations and foreign countries. So when we mention the "cost" to repeal WEP, GPO, and DE, let's not forget the corporate subsidies and the tax loopholes for the wealthy.

finance.yahoo.com/news/donald-trump-is-becoming-
wall-streets-best-friend-152323629.html# and
The Week, magazine Oct. 23, 2015 on p12

Cost to Eliminate the GPO / WEP

The only "cost" to the U.S. Government is the accrued interest due on the special issue Treasury bonds. The loan's principal is our money; our FICA contributions.

The SSA has projected that if the offsets were repealed the federal government would be required to repay the SS Trust Fund $6.2 billion per year for 10 years. So what! This was a known fact when the U.S. Government took our Trust Fund money and forced the Trust Fund to buy these specially issued "junk" bonds.

Compared to the *$364 billion* in subsides to the 288 corporations and the *$900 billion* every year in tax loopholes for the rich, the $62 billion one-time cost to repeal our offsets is chump change. If congress needs money to repeal the offsets than these subsides and tax loopholes would be a good place to start looking.

retirementsecurity.org/public/460.cfm

What is a "junk" bond?

**Junk bonds are so called because of their
higher default risk in relation
to investment-grade bonds.**

Nothing Contributed - Nothing Lost

All SS benefits are paid by current workers who pay FICA taxes. The Congress contributes NOTHING towards benefits, therefore, it's impossible for the government to lose. And, since the U.S. tax payers contribute NOTHING they cannot lose either.

Who Really Loses?

The "loss" is not to the government nor the taxpayers – it is to SS retirees like you and me. These are our earned benefits withheld as FICA taxes from us by the SSA who then uses offset penalties to legally deny us our benefits.

In 2004, the majority losing all or part of their benefits were women with a ratio of four women to each man affected. So it's ONLY you and I who are losing and paying this "cost."　　　　　www.ssa.gov/.../HRpt_072004.pdf 2004

If the federal government is finding the $6.2 billion per year is difficult to repay; then what about the $3 trillion it owes the Trust Fund?

Trump unnerved the financial industry during his campaign with his proposals to "remake the Fed and to repay debt at a discount if there's ever a crisis."

Finance.yahoo.com/news/Donald-trump-is-becoming-wall-street-s-best-friend-152323629.html#　May 18, 2016

Is our government expecting the Trust Fund to write off this debt or will the government discount or default on the loans as President Trump proposed during his campaign?

What does it mean to *discount the debt?*

It means that only a small amount of the $3 trillion dollars owed to the Trust Fund would be returned. The rest of the money would be written off as a "loss" or as a "bad" investment.

In other words, you and I lose a lot of money meant to pay our future SS benefits.

Above The Law

The *Sherman Antitrust Law* was enacted in 1890 a full 45 years before the Social Security Act of 1935. The Antitrust laws were aimed at business entities and insurance firms. Although exempt, the Social Security Administration should not be managing our "social insurance" Trust Fund monies outside of and above the law.

The concept of competition, or lack thereof, is demonstrated by the "closed to competition" SS retirement system created by Congress which forces all workers to pay into an inefficient investment sinkhole run by the Commissioner.

While the Illinois Supreme Court decision, *2015 IL 118585,* confirmed that state pension benefits are constitutionally guaranteed -- our SS benefits are NOT guaranteed.

President Obama 2016

"I think Congress has been stuck, partly for ideological reasons, in taking some common sense steps that would improve the economy and help working families.

Competition is good for consumers,"
"That's the way the free market works."

"The more competition we have, the more products, services, (and) innovation take(s) place."

Obama on Yahoo Finance April 15, 2016

On April 15, 2016 President Barack Obama signed an executive order directing every relevant agency of the Federal government to take steps in identifying bottlenecks to competition and to create new ways to increase competition in the economy.

The executive order put agencies on a fast-track path to, within 60 days, identify the steps they would take.

Certain practices such as collusion, and anticompetitive exclusionary conduct stifle competition and erode the foundation of America's economic vitality. Obama said this executive action focusing on consumer issues is key for leveling the playing field.

The report pointed to efficiencies of scale and how workers and consumers would benefit from additional policy actions by the government to promote competition.

The Council of Economic Advisors (CEA) released a report that documented evidence that competition has been reduced in the economy.

If the SSA was seriously trying to help prevent a Trust Fund shortage, the cost/benefit analysis, from which they are currently exempt, would be embraced.

obama-executive-order-competition-093636744

Overview of The Antitrust Laws

Congress passed the first antitrust law, the *Sherman Act,* in 1890 as a "comprehensive charter of economic liberty aimed at preserving free and unfettered competition as the rule of trade."   In 1914, Congress passed two additional antitrust laws: the *Federal Trade Commission Act,* which created the FTC, and the *Clayton Act.*

With some revisions, the following are the three core federal antitrust laws still in effect today:

1. The Sherman Act outlaws "every contract, combination, or conspiracy in restraint of trade."   And any "monopolization, attempted monopolization, or conspiracy or combination to monopolize." On the other hand, certain acts are considered so harmful to competition that they are almost always illegal.

These acts are "*per se*" violations of the Sherman Act; in other worlds, no defense or justification is allowed. The penalties for violation of the Sherman Act can be severe. The Supreme Court has said that all violations of the Sherman Act also violates the FTC.

2. The Federal Trade Commission Act is the primary statute of the Commission. Under this Act, the Commission is empowered, among other things, to:

(a) **prevent unfair methods of competition, and unfair or deceptive acts or practices in or affecting commerce;**

(b) **seek monetary redress and other relief for conduct injurious to consumers;**

(c) **make reports and legislative recommendations to Congress.**

Only the FTC brings cases under the FTC Act.

3. Bureau of Consumer Protection As the nation's consumer protection agency, the FTC takes complaints about businesses that don't make good on their promises or cheat people out of money. They share these complaints with law enforcement partners and use them to investigate fraud and eliminate unfair business practices.

ftc.gov/enforcement/anticompetitive-practices

Unfair Methods of Competition The FTC takes action to stop and prevent unfair business practices that are likely to reduce competition and lead to higher prices, reduced quality or levels of service, or less innovation.

The FTC generally pursues anticompetitive conduct as violations of Section 5 of the Federal Trade Commission Act.

The Clayton Act Section 7 of the Clayton Act prohibits mergers and acquisitions where the effect "may be substantially to lessen competition, or to tend to create a monopoly."

Section 5: 15 U.S.C. § 45(a)(1). The ban on unfair methods of competition encompasses not only those acts and practices that violate the Sherman or Clayton Act but also those that contravene the spirit of the antitrust laws and those that, if allowed to mature or complete, could violate the Sherman or Clayton Act.

Anticompetitive practices include activities like exclusionary exclusive dealing contracts into two types:

Single Firm Conduct -- It is unlawful for a company to monopolize or attempt to monopolize trade, meaning a firm with market power cannot act to maintain or acquire a dominant position by excluding competitors or preventing new entry.

It is important to note that it is not illegal for a company to have a monopoly, to charge "high prices," or to try to achieve a monopoly position by aggressive methods. A company violates the law only if it tries to maintain or acquire a monopoly through unreasonable methods.

Horizontal Conduct -- It is illegal for businesses to act together in ways that can limit competition, lead to higher prices, or hinder other businesses from entering the market. The FTC challenges unreasonable horizontal restraints of trade.

Such agreements may be considered unreasonable when competitors interact to such a degree that they are no longer acting independently, or when collaborating gives competitors the ability to wield market power together. Certain acts are considered so harmful to competition that they are almost always illegal. These include arrangements to fix prices, divide markets, or rig bids.

Breach of Contract -- If you believe that the policy states they should do something or pay for the benefits you have claimed, but they have denied your claim, then this is a claim for breach.

This means they did not perform their obligations under the contract of insurance.

Bad Faith In PA, there is a law, 42 Pa CS Section 8371 et seq, that requires your insurance company to treat you with *good faith and fair dealing*. They cannot knowingly act unreasonably and recklessly disregard the fact that they are acting unreasonably.   Examples:

1. denying your claim despite clear facts indicating they should pay it;

2. misrepresenting the terms and conditions of the policy;

3. unreasonable refusal to pay proceeds of a policy

U.S Supreme Court

Courts apply the antitrust laws to changing markets and for over 100 years, the antitrust laws have had the same basic objective to protect the process to benefit consumers.

> "to protect the process of competition for the benefit of consumers, making sure there are strong incentives to operate efficiently."

The U.S. Supreme Court held that the Sherman Act, applies to insurance.

The Court held that insurance could be regulated by the U.S. Congress under the Commerce Clause.

*Congress responded by enacting
the McCarran-Ferguson Act of 1945
to exempt the SSA
from the antitrust laws.*

15 U.S.C. §§ 1011-1015

The McCarran–Ferguson Act The Act provides that federal antitrust laws will NOT apply to the "business of insurance" as long as *the state-regulates* in that area, but federal anti-trust laws will apply in cases of boycott, coercion, and intimidation.

**Since states do not regulate the SSA,
the SSA,
with the help of Congress,
side-stepped the
antitrust Sherman Act.**

Why should the SSA be
treated differently
when it comes to the law?

And which law

is protecting the rights

of SS retirees?

Chapter 10

Challenging the SSA

𝒫erhaps the first time you heard about SS offsets, was when you applied for SS. If your SS benefit will have an offset withheld, you have what is called an "*unfavorable determination.*" This means you have the right to appeal. The SS appeal process is FREE, and you do not need an attorney. You may appeal your offset by filing your appeal with the SS clerk in your local office or online. You may refer to the POMS regulation number that governs the issue, but it is not necessary.

The appeal review usually takes place at your local SS office where you present your case to an ALJ Judge via a video conference. Your hearing will be monitored and recorded and usually lasts about an hour.

When it comes to appealing your determination you must be prepared and should have your questions written down. Many of the issues you may want to challenge are covered in Chapter 11 and the appeal process is covered in Chapter 12. You may request a hard copy version of your hearing -- which is normally free.

**Remember, if you
do not appeal,
your silence
is your consent.**

Boiling A Frog

You have probably heard that you can cook a frog to death by putting it in a pot of water and heating the water slowly. The frog will just sit as the water begins to boil. The frog then cooks and dies. So it is with the SS offsets, as one person at a time loses a portion of their benefits, and like the frog, they usually sit, boiling mad but doing nothing.

We can pressure Congress and demand the offsets be repealed. Remember, only Congress and the President have the power to repeal the offset regulations.

It Takes Just One

Most grass root protests start with a single person or a group determined to change a wrong. All it takes to get the all rolling is a common goal and a leader to rally others into action. Many people may feel the same as you, but they are unable to act without the support and guidance of a leader. Joining a group may be more comfortable for them, and large groups complaining send a very powerful message to Congress.

We need to stop the "every man for himself" fragmented approach when protesting to Congress. Groups can solve the "divide and conquer" problem by joining others to protest the offsets.

Appendix C lists many organizations you can join for free. Many "How to Protest" web sites are on the internet and explain how to go about starting a protest movement. Congress takes notice when many voices are barking in their ear demanding action. So start barking!

The important thing is to speak up at meetings; talk to co-workers or have open discussions at your home, church or library to discuss the issues your group may want to challenge. Facebook, Twitter, YouTube and blogs are also a great way to connect with others dealing with offsets.

The Rosa Parks Story

On December 1, 1955, after a long day's work at a Montgomery department store, Rosa Parks boarded the Cleveland Avenue bus for home. She refused to sit in the back of the bus, and her challenge was a media success simply by bringing to the nation an awareness of the Civil Rights Movement.

She said, "The only thing that bothered me was that we waited so long to make this protest."

"There were times when it would have been easy...to go in the opposite direction, but somehow I felt that if I took one more step someone would come along to join me."

Rosa Parks, December 1, 1955

www.biography.com/people/rosa-parks-9433715#
montgomery-bus-boycott

Where To Begin

You begin your challenge with the issues that are important to you. Then take action.

Write emails, or use other digital methods to write to your Representatives and the President. Address only one issue per email and keep it to one page. When you write your own self-styled email, it will receive greater attention from the staff than if you use a form letter.

State what needs to change. When you challenge a POMS regulation, state <u>exactly why</u> it is unfair or discriminatory towards you, a surviving spouse, minorities, mothers, etc. Keep it short and be very specific.

What action do you want? Explain exactly what <u>action you</u> <u>are requesting </u>your representatives or union officials to undertake. Do you want the law, rewritten, income exemptions added or an item repealed?

Send   monthly   emails   to   your   Congressional Representatives,   but   do   not   overwhelm   your Representative with daily emails. Too many emails on the same subject, from the same person, will numb the receiver and lose their attention.

Remember, the pen is
mightier than the sword.

How To Eat an Elephant

How to eat an elephant – one bite at a time and so it is with the offsets.   Rather than asking Congress to repeal an entire   WEP, GPO, or DE offset regulation, it may be a smarter strategy to divide the offset issues into smaller bite size pieces. Changing one small section may be easier for Congress to swallow than grouping everything into one large hard-to-digest request.   This also works   when challenging your state's pension plan policies.

Keep in mind the final goal is to repeal all offsets -- but if you can change only a small section or have even one law rewritten, it's a success and will open the door for more changes. Success will come slowly. Day by day, by challenging one item at a time, Congress may eventually be persuaded to repeal these unfair offsets.

Contacting Your Representatives

Make personal phone calls to your Representatives and Senators and leave comments on their web site to bring attention to your offset concerns. To find the name and information for your congressional representative(s) go to the following web sites: *www.house.gov* or *www.senate.gov,* type in the name of your state to find the information on each representative, his or her mail address, phone and web site.

You may also check on current bills in Congress regarding WEP, GPO, or Dual Entitlement by going to: **waysandmeans.house.gov/committeesubmissions wep gpo.**

Snail Mail & Social Media

Snail mail is okay, but members of Congress and the President have their snail mail screened and x-rayed by security who is searching for harmful toxins and chemicals. This screening takes time, and your letter may take 2-3 months before it is delivered to your Representative.

To avoid the long delay, email and Twitter are the preferred contact methods. The White House has said that, emails and Twitter were the fastest way to contact the President whose email is

president@whitehouse.gov

An individual can be quite effective with their own email campaign. Once you start tweeting or emailing you will find you can do it quickly and it also becomes easier. So keep writing Congress and ask them to repeal the offset regulations.

Your Local Library

Your local library is a great place to reach the public. You could give your local library a copy of this book. Most libraries would also like you to promote the book by stimulating the public's interest.

Remember, if a book is in the library for two to three months and is seldom checked out, the low interest and lack of demand signals the library to remove the book from the shelf and sell it in their used book department

One way you can generate interest is to offer free seminars at various times, mornings, afternoons, nights, etc. Also have a flier outlining the times and topics available at the library information desk.

You could mail or hand deliver fliers to your police, fire, teachers, and other city workers announcing your upcoming seminars. Also, offer to present a seminar at their work site to make it convenient for workers not close to a library.

You could also give each group a book for their employee's lounge, with your contact information written inside.

Give each attendee a blank index card and ask them to write down their questions for a discussion session at the end of the seminar, or offer to contact them personally during the week. Have a sign-in registry with a request for the attendee's email address to aid you in contacting them later with updates.

Each seminar could focus on one of the offsets. WEP could be for one week, GPO the next, etc.

Keep your seminars <u>short</u> about- 1 hour

TV, Radio and Newspapers

Along with promoting upcoming free seminars at your local library you might try a few blips on your local TV and radio stations. Perhaps send a short local-interest article to the newspaper announcing your upcoming seminars.

Groups, Unions & Organizations

If you belong to a union, giving a seminar at a meeting would be a good way to get your union members involved.

Union officials do not like the offsets either, as they create unhappy members.

Inform current and younger workers that they, too, will be caught in the offset pension-grab when they retire. Offer to send union members emails about upcoming seminars. In addition to your own challenges, joining and supporting various organizations, such as *ssfairness.com* via their email campaigns will add to the demand for Congress to take action.   see **Appendix C for organizations.**

Petitions

Petitions are great and they get results, but your petition needs to address specific issues. If you have a local group, then by all means draft a list of each issue along with the action you wish your Representatives to undertake. It helps to sign these petitions, but don't stop there. Write your own emails and send them specifically to your State Representatives, and the President. And, if what you're doing is not working try something else. Check out these web sites: change.org/start-a-petition,   and
            thepetitionsite.com/useful-community-development.org/

Kevin Brady and Richard Neal

Here is a sample of how the Texas union members, working together, approached their Representatives.

In November of 2015, two members of Congress, Representative Kevin Brady, Rep. of Texas, and Representative Richard Neal, Dem. of Massachusetts, introduced *H.R. 5697, the Equal Treatment of Public Servants Act.*   kevinbrady.house.gov 11/13/15

In a **press release**, Representative Brady stated:

> "Our goal for many years has been to END the unfair WEP and provide equal treatment to all workers in Social Security, including our teachers, firefighters, police and other public servants who have contributed into Social Security."

What Happened Next?

The bill was referred to the House Committee on Ways and Means, a committee on which Representative Brady serves. After review by the Committee, the bill would need to be brought to the House of Representatives for a vote.

Then if passed, it would need to be presented to the Senate for a vote as well. If the bill passes both Houses of Congress, it would then be sent to the President to be signed into law or vetoed.

waysandmeans.house.gov/committeesubmissions

While the news was good, there was much work to be done to get H.R. 5697 passed! Texas Retired Teachers Association, TRTA, launched an email advocacy campaign on this issue with their Texas Congressional Delegation.

For now, TRTA members have spread the word to their fellow retirees and their friends in the active school community that they have not given up on the idea of fairness for their members and their Social Security earnings. They are gearing up!

Follow them on Twitter or Facebook!   Visit their YouTube channel for regular video updates. To read the transcript go to: .govtrack.us/congress/bills/113/hr569

This approach, in Texas, could also work in your state. It is an outrage that these federal benefit formulas treat civil servants pensions as if they were *some sort of ill-gotten gain* and that civil servants must be financially "equalized."

Teacher Shortages

Many states are losing thousands of teachers each year, and the states which subject their teachers to the penalties of WEP and GPO, will find it increasingly difficult to fill the vacant positions. Offsets only exacerbate the situation as school employees and other public servants nationwide lose billions of dollars a year to offset penalties.

Boycotts

Workers could boycott civil positions in the 28 states with offset penalties. Current and new employees need to know that the job they are working in, or about to accept, will cause them to lose all or most of their SS benefits. Get your union to join in the boycotts and insist that civil servants should not be singled out for offsets.

Working in a Government job often

puts you at risk of

losing your Social Security benefits.

Two million American retirees have had their

hard-earned benefits partially

cut or completely eliminated.

Who's on Your Side
Democrats vs Republicans-

On December 17, 2015 the Yahoo finance web page ran an article called *"How Democrats and Republicans differ on Social Security"*, written by Alicia H. Munnell of the Center for Retirement Research at Boston College.   She wrote:

Democrats: would rely on increasing revenues and benefits to correct income inequality.

Republicans: would take the opposite approach and raise the full retirement age and reduce benefits for all workers.

The Republicans whose main focus is on getting government "out of our lives" sounds very appealing. Republicans say government is too big, too intrusive and there is too much welfare spending.

If you believe *eliminating* unemployment insurance, food stamps, heating assistance, rent subsidies, Medicare, Medicaid and Social Security along with other government programs is a good thing then we are going to further increase income inequality. We need our government to help low-income retirees, the disabled, those in poverty, and the homeless.

Removing these safety nets is a stupid idea.

Robert Reich Said:

"If we are to reduce government then Congress needs to stop the *huge subsidies* paid to oil companies, corporate farms and to foreign countries. These subsidies are going mostly to wealthy corporations but I have not heard of anyone in congress calling for the elimination of these taxpayer funded give-away programs."

Robert Reich, former Secretary of Labor, went on to say for example: "most condemn what they called 'crony capitalism,' by which they mean big corporations getting *sweetheart deals from the government* because of lobbying and campaign contributions."

"I met with a group of small farmers in Missouri who were livid about the growth of 'factory farms' owned and run by big corporations, that abuse land and cattle, damage the environment, and ultimately harm consumers."

They claimed giant food processors were using their monopoly power to squeeze the farmers dry, and the government was doing squat about it because of Big Agriculture's money."   **www.robertreich.org 11/08/2015**

Robert Reich wrote *Beyond Outrage*
and is co-creator of the award-winning
documentary, *Inequality For All* , now on DVD.

The Costly Migration

What money the SSA is saving today using WEP, GPO, and DE offset penalties, becomes an expense to another agency tomorrow. If you close the front door, the retirees will go through the back door. Retirees do NOT disappear, their needs do NOT disappear, and their living expenses do NOT disappear.

Endless forms and repetitive paperwork does not slow down the rising tide of SS recipients who now must migrate to other agencies to get the financial help they need. These recipients are joining the millions already swamping the programs which help our low income citizens.

Chasing Shadows

It hard to understand how Congress can possibly believe that placing obstacles and hurdles for seniors to jump over, climb through or crawl around slows down or solves the Trust Fund shortage. Congress and the SSA are chasing shadows while at the same time they are increasing the bitterness felt towards them by our retired public servants.

The SSA seems to believe that if they use public servants as scapegoats, apply offsets to their SS pensions, the forecasted shortage in the SS Trust Fund would magically disappear or be vastly reduced.

Sorry, but this is delusional thinking.

It's like pouring water from one glass to another,

the amount of water is the same it just ends up

in a different glass. In our example,

the retired cash-strapped

seniors just migrate to other agencies for financial help.

Like the water in the glass,

nothing changes,

except which agency

must now

deal with the expense.

Cost shifting is not the answer!

Chapter 11

Issues To Appeal

𝔖he following are some issues:

The Only Game in Town

In the Social Security game of benefit determinations, investments, and offset penalties, only the SSA and the SS Trustees get to play. The SSA has complete control and your FICA tax is mandatory without other retirement investment plans or options.

The SSA alone makes the decisions as to how many years are used in calculating your benefits, and at what age, you must be to receive your full retirement benefits. Your beneficiary is predetermined by the SSA and are only two options – your spouse or your children. The SSA keeps all your contributions, decides your benefit amount, and on top of that they buy, the proven safe but poor performing, special issue Treasury bonds.

We need investment choices similar to those offered in a 401 (k) and beneficiary options

You may want to review the Brookings Institution report on:

"How Would Investing in Equities Have Affected the Social Security Trust Fund?"

This report helps to explain why and what is being done to loosen the vise-grip that the SSA and Congress has on our SS benefits and the Trust Fund investments.

www.brookings.edu/contact-brookings

An Unequal Penalty

The Social Security WEP offset formula favors the highest paid workers who have 30 or more years of substantial earnings. These favored retirees do NOT PAY a WEP offset penalty.

The substantial formula severely penalizes most women, part-time or seasonal workers, minorities and those with a lifetime of low wages.

www.ssa.gov/pubs/EN-05-10045.pdf. 2017

The WEP formula is upside down. This happens because of the huge drop in the percentage rate from 90% for those with less than 30 years of substantial SS earnings to a low of 40% for those workers with less than 20 years.

The 2017 Highest-Paid Workers:

LESS than 30 years of substantial earnings.

Tier 1	90%	of first	**$10,620**	**$ 9,558**
Tier 2	32%	between	**$10,620 - $64,032**	**$17,091**
Tier 3	15%	over	**$64,032** & up to but not over	**$ 5,595**

Maximum 2017 SS benefit is $2,687
Average male   in 2014 received $1,425.50
Average female in 2014 received $1,095.83

The 2017 Low-Wage Workers:

LESS than 20 years of substantial earnings.

Tier 1	40%	of first	**$10,620**	**$4,248**
Tier 2	32%	between	**$10,620 – $64,032**	**$6,179**

Average 2016 SS for low-wage worker $869
Average SS earnings $29,930 for 50% of workers.

If Tier 1 was 90% for the low wage
earner instead of 40%
the worker would receive $1,311
or $442 more per month.

To find the 2016 average WEP offset amount for the
SS years worked ranging from
20 to 29 see the following chart.
www.socialsecurity.gov/retire2/wep-chart.htm.

Or search SSA Pub. #05-10045 January 2017

Because more than half of all workers, 84 million earn
$29,930 per year or less -- they never reach Tier 3.

The poor get poorer.

For every year less than 30, down to 20 years your WEP
offset penalty increases by 5%, but it never goes lower
than 40%. However, at 40%, your monthly SS benefit is
less than half that of the high paid worker.

The less you earn the larger your WEP penalty

By working part-time in a low paying government job, many
of these workers were trying to add a second pension to
their small SS retirement check. Instead, they will lose up
to $3 from their SS check for every $1 they receive as a
government pension. They, unknowingly, were and many
are still working themselves into greater poverty.

The low-income workers, unable to pass the substantial
earnings test, are severely punished
with the highest offset deductions.

wages $29,930 www.ssa.gov/cgi-in/netcomp.cgi?year=2015   and
obliviousinvestor.com/how-social-security-benefits-are-calculated

One corrective action could be to have the offset rate fixed at 10% for everyone so that everyone, regardless of income, will receive the 90% rate in Tier 1. Another option would be to have an offset exemption for those with 30 years of low earnings and a low retirement income.

SSA Substantial Earnings Pub No. 05-10045

If we cannot repeal this terrible law, then make the offset deduction percentage the same for everyone.

Grandfather Clause Needed

The SSA needs a grandfather clause to end the robbing of the worker who was caught midway in their career by the offset regulations. Who ever heard of a regulation this financially destructive not having a grandfather clause? And, why doesn't it?

Offset regulations went into effect in 1983, but our government did NOT require workers be notified until after 2004. The workers, who applied for benefits prior to 2004, were caught completely unaware and dumbfounded when they learned of their WEP offset penalties and again when under the GPO, many would lose every dollar of their spousal SS.

Congress needs to add a grandfather clause to all offset regulations.

A Low-Income Means Test

Offsets were meant to equalize all retirees, says the SSA. But how is "equalizing" an impoverished retiree with crushing offsets fair? In many state and government welfare programs, your income determines your benefits. The SSA should be doing the same income determination, before it deducts offset penalties from the poor.

There needs to be an offset exemption for low income retirees.

The Death Benefit & Beneficiaries

The one-time pitiful $255 death benefit is a joke. The death benefit needs to be increased to $10,000 or more and be increased each year to keep up with inflation.

The death benefit needs to cover the expenses of a basic funeral.

Currently, the SSA regulations state that only your married spouse or your child is eligible to be your beneficiary. If you do not have an eligible beneficiary, the SSA keeps your death benefit.

This narrow self-serving SS regulation needs to be updated to give you the right to choose your beneficiaries. You should be allowed to have more than one beneficiary, perhaps other family members; a friend; a church; or a charity.

We should be allowed to choose our beneficiaries

Transitional Death Benefits

The sudden discontinuation of a deceased spouse's SS check puts untold hardship and stress on the surviving spouse. The expenses for the funeral and costs to settle the estate usually fall on the surviving spouse or child. As it is now, many surviving spouses' face a 100% GPO offset, and will not receive a SS survivor benefit.

The spouse, or child, needs help and should continue to receive the deceased's full SS check for two or more years. Today, without a substantial death benefit, the surviving spouse faces a large funeral expense and the immediate loss of their spouse's SS check, all at once. These two very stressful events occur at a time when the survivor must quickly adjust to a low-income life style.

The SS needs to provide transitional benefits.

Stop the Life Expectancy Modification

The SSA is greedy and using LE "modifications" to rip-off retirees. Today a 65-year-old man can expect to live another 21 years and a woman, the same age, can expect to live another 23 years, yet the SS has "modified" both his and her life expectancies down to 10 years.

See POMS RS 00605.364 in Appendix E .p. 240

Your "modified," or reduced, life expectancy causes a doubling and even tripling of your monthly offset deduction. The younger you are when you take your lump sum the more likely your monthly offset deduction will triple.

**The SS should use our
real life expectancy
and stop the "modifications."**

You should ask your SS office to explain how they have determined your LE. Show them a copy of *Actuarial Studies, 2000s - Social Security Study No. 120,* and how your LE differs from the *POMS Lifetime Chart RS 00605.364.* Finally, request an *Appeal for Reconsideration* form.

ssa.gov/oact/NOTES/s2000s.html

Lower the Full Retirement Age

Instead of increasing the full retirement age, the SSA should lower it to encourage more seniors to retire. Social Security benefits, however, are so inadequate that many seniors cannot afford to retire at any age. If they had a larger SS benefit, many seniors would retire.

The SSA is too stingy! Benefits could easily be increased by 50% or more to give all retired seniors a decent standard of living. Given the huge maximum FICA taxes of $600,000 paid during our working years, a 50% increase is reasonable.

The average SS benefit for March 2017 was $1,250, down from $1,341 in 2016. SS benefits could easily increase to $1875 and the SS would still have a $150,000 surplus.

ssa.gov/policy410-965-0090 statistics@ssa.gov

SS benefits need to increase.

A COLA Guarantee

Why should we retirees have to hold our breath every year waiting for the announcement of our yearly COLA increase? The special issue Treasury bond investments enable a CPA accountant to calculate the yearly cash flows for the next 10 or 20 years and they could just as easily forecast the potential inflation and COLA increases for the next 2 to 5 years as well.

The Colorado PERA pension agency guarantees a 2% COLA increase or more every year. Congress could require that the SSA provide a similar guarantee with a bonus check in an exceptionally high-inflationary year.

> **SS retirees need a guaranteed minimum yearly COLA increase.**

Substantial Earnings, Why 30 Years?

Under current law, a worker's offset penalty is based on the substantial earnings test. If you have, 30 years or more, you will not have an offset deduction. However, if you have less than 30 years you will pay an offset penalty.

Because women often take years off from their careers to raise children, and perhaps need to care for their elderly parents, many women fail the substantial earnings requirement. The average woman has SS earnings credits for only 27 years.

By using 35 years of earnings, even when indexed, pulls down your final yearly average. Your low earnings average then results in you receiving a small SS benefit.

In Colorado, the PERA pension averages only the three highest earning years, not 35, which then give the state government retirees a generous pension. The SS's thirty-five years is excessive, is unfair, and is an overkill. SS should also be using only our highest 3-5 earning years for our SS determination.

The substantial earnings test needs be eliminated. The SSA should use only our highest 3-5 years of earnings.

The State "Matching" Trap

States that require you to accept the "matching money" on your lump sum withdrawal trigger your offsets. This is a big problem and yet an easy one to fix. Refusing the "matching funds" usually will stop all your offsets, but only if it is NOT your main retirement plan.

The term "match" is incorrect because what the SS and the state call "matching funds" are actually your capital gains, dividends, and interest earned on your contributions.

The state wants to hire and retain its civil servants so the state agency has no incentive to reveal the negatives in their pension plan. When you read the offset information they provide, you may find the information is vague and skimpy.

You may find that petitioning directly to your state pension agency and officials requesting the "matching funds" rule be changed may be quicker and easier than asking Congress for offset repeal.

> **If your state's pension plan forces its members to take the "matching funds"-- then protest! We need the right to refuse the match.**

Appendix B has state agency contact information.
Appendix E has the full version of the POMS RS 00605.364 regulation.

An Offset End Date

SSA Administrative Law Judge Olson's decision, in the SS appeal, stated that the number in the *POMS RS 00605.364 Life Time Table* was NOT a person's life expectancy, but rather the expected life of a lump sum. Judge Olson said: at age 55; the lump sum would last 140.9 months.

Therefore, in his decision there was a positive "*yes*" to the question asking if the offsets had an ending date. Judge Olson stated, "Once the lump sum had been depleted there would no longer be a pension, therefore, no offsets and the SS benefits should then be 100% restored."

The SSA, then said "sorry, the answer is *no*" -- the lump sum would never be depleted; and, the offsets would never end.

The SSA claimed Judge Olson made an
"error in law" and overturned his decision.

At the end of the 140.9 months the SS said the offsets would begin again and continue to repeat over and over using the same LE modification to double the offset deduction every month. These offset deductions would be taken forever – they would never end.

Remember, this highly inflated offset amount was determined by reducing they life expectancy at age 55, from 31.7 years to 12.6 years.

Life Tables U.S. 1995-Con. Is in Appendix E

We need to petition Congress to stop using this "modified" lifetime table as a life expectancy chart. The SSA needs to agree that it is the depletion schedule of the lump sum which t does have an ending date.

Congress needs to stop the
never-ending offset deductions.

We need the ending date.

Unobtainable Fixed Returns

The SSA expects the 2005 lump sum would be fully invested and earning a permanent 6% fixed rate of return forever and ever regardless of the current interest rate. The SSA also never allows for withdrawals from this sum be incorporated into their calculation.

How can the lump sum still have the same amount invested forever, if a person has been taking a monthly withdrawal? After the full 140.9 months of offset deductions has been reached, the original lump sum balance would drop to zero. This is then the ending date and the date when your SS benefits should be restored 100& -- to the full amount.

:

Why is the SSA NOT using a depletion schedule and recalculating
a new lump sum balance each month?

If the SSA Trust Fund investments earn a little over 1%, how does the SSA justify calculating a 2005 lump sum payout at 6%?

Why is the 6% rate never adjusted?

The interest rate needs to be updated each year to mirror the 10-year Treasury bill rate.

SS Credits

You should be angry when the SSA takes all of your lump sum pension money, yet does not give you a SS earnings credit.

What is so infuriating is that Congress, with all their amendments, has never addressed this issue. The SSA guts a retiree's state pension and yet they are not required to give these government retirees any SS earnings credits? The question is -- why not?

**Congress needs to correct the
earnings credit oversight.**

SSA Contribution Refunds

The SSA keeps all your FICA contributions and your share of the earnings on the bond investments. If you die before applying for your SS benefits or should you fail to meet the required 40 quarters of work, you may never receive a SS pension.

**The SSA should be required to refund all of the
FICA taxes by those people who fall short of the
40 quarters, or die before collecting.**

Annuities give their clients a "time certain" clause, which means that if they should die within a certain period, usually 10 to 20 years, their heirs would receive the remaining monthly payments in the time certain period.

In the Colorado state pension, PERA, the agency will refund all your contributions plus the earnings in a one-time lump sum payment if you fail to meet the eligibility requirements for a state pension.

The SS however, gives nothing back.

We need refunds for those who die or fail to meet the eligibility requirement.

Why a 10-Year Marriage Rule?

A 10-year marriage should not be a qualifying requirement for claiming SS benefits on the earnings of your partner.

Like many SS regulations, it is mainly women who get short-changed.

The years of unpaid work in the home gives them no SS earnings credits.

If your spouse fails to be married to you for 10 years or more, they will not receive one cent from the SS as a spousal benefit. It is time for the SS to modernize and be harmony with today's many lifestyles. Every year that you are married should earn you SS credits towards a spousal pension or as credits to your own SS account. Currently, it is all or nothing at all -- you either have 10 full years of marriage or you do not. One month less than 10 years, and you will receive nothing from the SSA.

**The 10-year marriage requirement
needs to be updated.**

Motherhood Penalty

In 1997, the Dual Entitlement rule slashed the benefits of more than 5.6 million women. The "motherhood penalty" is identical to the working spouse who also receives nothing extra in return for their years of work, but instead receives the same SS benefit amount as the spouse who never worked.

Jon Forman "The Taxman" published in The Journal Record
[of Oklahoma City], July 14, 2000

The problem with the Social Security DE rule is that it punishes the working mother by keeping all of her FICA contributions but gives her no additional benefits. These women should get a full refund of all their FICA taxes or be entitled to receive both their own SS benefit in addition to their spousal benefit.

jay.law.ou.edu/faculty/jforman/Opeds/jr8-00(SS-working-mothers).htm

Congress needs to reward working women
with extra SS benefits, not take their
FICA contributions and
give them nothing in return.

Gender Inequality

The SSA treats women more unfairly than any other group.

The following are some issues affecting mainly women:

With women earning only 80% for every dollar a man earns
and only 66% for their work in -skilled occupations, seems
only fair to have two formulas for the substantial earnings test.

The SS should index women's earnings at a higher
ratio because of the gender pay gap.

The SS should reduce the averaged earnings to three years of
your highest earning years instead of the 35 years.

The 10-year marriage requirement needs to change
to a graduated spousal SS benefit
percentage for every year married

We need an offset exemption for those
with low monthly incomes.

The spousal GPO should NOT take more than 50% of a
spouses survival benefit. WEP and GPO should be the same.

The offset rate needs to be the same for everyone,
not a 90% rate for the wealthy and
a 40% rate for the poor.

It's regressive now with women and minorities
receiving less than half of their SS pension money
at the Tier 1 level as the richer retiree

Why Only One CPI for All?

A single CPI does not work.

Our basic needs and purchases change as we age.

For seniors, health care is their largest expense.

Apwu.org/news/deptdiv-news/article/sen-elizabeth-warren

We need a senior CPI that would reflect more accurately the goods and services that seniors buy or use.

Elizabeth Warren

Elizabeth Warren's, D-MA, response to the no-COLA for 2016, was to introduce *Bill #S2251 called Seniors and Veterans Emergency Benefits Act* requesting a one-time payment of $581 to all SS beneficiaries. The lame excuse the SS used to explain why there would be no COLA increase for 2016 was that the price of gas went down! This drop in the price of gas was your COLA increase said the SS. Appears this bill just disappeared into a black hole.

Elizabeth Warren said, "We can afford to give seniors and vets a raise. In fact, we can increase pay for seniors and vets without adding a single penny to the deficit simply by closing the bonus loophole for corporate executives."

Elizabeth Warren, D-MA said:

"Projections for the costs of core goods and services show inflation is up about 2%, but seniors won't get a cost of living increase – mostly because of falling gasoline prices, which don't mean as much to millions of seniors who don't commute to work."

Why?

It's NOT an accident.
It's NOT inevitable.
It's the result of deliberate policies set by Congress.

cnn.com/2015/11/11/opionions/warren-social-security-recipients-deserve-raise ⁓ Elizabeth Warren 11/11/15

COLA for 2017

Millions of Social Security beneficiaries received a meager 0.39% COLA increase in 2017.

The 0.39 percent COLA increase for 2017 was about $4.00 per month for each retiree.

Jacob Lew, Trustee for Social Security Trust Fund

WASHINGTON (AP)
"Meager hike in Social Security benefits next year."
by Stephen Ohlemacher & Rocardp Alonso-Zaldiver

The Obama administration on December 8, 2016, issued
a 2.1% pay raise for federal employees that started in 2017,
while you and I got a skimpy 0.39% COLA.

www.govexec.com/pay-benefits/..2107..federal-pay-raise 12/08/16

In more grim news, the trustees said that some Medicare
beneficiaries would face sharply higher Part B premiums
for outpatient care.

Treasury Secretary Steve Mnuchin

Annual Board of Trustees Report

on Social Security and Medicare.

June 2017

You may **Email Steve Mnuchin**

www.treasury.gov/connect/Pages/Message-to-the-Secretary.aspx

The Goal

The goal is to have all offsets repealed.
And it would be nice if all the past offset
penalties were refunded to recipients
retroactive to the day they
applied for SS benefits.

We do not need one regulation for the rich
and another for the rest of us.

Without demanding

change;

nothing will change.

These are just a few of the issues to consider.

If you have other issues,

please email them to: **ssoffsets@yahoo.com**

Chapter 12

Filing An Appeal

You have the right to appeal if you do not like your offset determination. All SS appeals are FREE, and you may appeal at any time even if you have been receiving SS for years.

Your SSA office will give you a *"Request for Reconsideration" Form, SSA-561-U2,* which you may fill out at home. The appeals process may be found online at:
www.ssa.gov/appeals. SS publication EN-05-10041

Be sure to list each complaint on this form. This is important, because should you appeal to an Administrative Law Judge, ALJ, you may not change, add, or remove any issues from your original complaint. However, you may add supporting details.

Always make a hard copy for your records before mailing, or hand delivering, the completed form to your local SSA office.

> **If you're angered at the outrageously unending offset deductions with no compensating Social Security credits - then appeal.**

On Your Own

Once you begin the appeal process, your local office will be instructed not to engage in any conversations with you regarding your appeal. This lack of help can be infuriating, but any conversations could be construed as providing you with legal advice. The SS office staff, however, will help you fill out and provide you with the correct forms and will fax, for free, your documents.

This appeal process may seem scary, but you have nothing to lose, and you are quite capable of representing yourself.

Your Appeal Meeting

The SSA will notify you by snail-mail the time and place for your appeal meeting. Usually it will be a casual meeting with a SS representative at your local office. It would be wise to bring a written list of your questions and if possible have a witness present to listen and observe.

You may find the SS representative will not change the determination, which is quite common. You are then entitled to proceed to the next level.

The next level will bring your case before an Administrative Law Judge, ALJ. You will fill out a form called: *"Request for Hearing by Administrative Law Judge"*, HA 501-U5. On the form you will be asked to answer the following statement, *"I disagree with the determination made on my claim because:"*

This request will get your complaint on record and in the SS database. You have a right to ask how your offsets are determined, exactly how they are calculated and if they have an ending date.

However, because this is only a request,
you could be denied a hearing

Hearing by Administrative Law Judge

If your request is granted you will receive a snail-mailed letter from the SSA informing you of when and where your hearing will be held. Your hearing may be conducted via a video conference and it will be recorded.

Once your appeal has been heard, the ALJ will issue a written decision and snail-mail you a copy. In most cases, you will need to sign for this letter at your local post office. The SSA will provide you with a CD and a written transcript free of charge, if requested.

The Administrative Law Judge, if he or she rules in your favor, can reverse your offset determination.

NOTE: The SS ALJ operates independently of the agency even though they technically work for the SSA.

Faxes and Registered Mail

During your appeal, you may find the SSA will state that their office never received anything from you. To avoid this pitfall, always fax your documents using your local SSA office and request the original confirmation printout from the SS clerk.

The clerk needs to write a short statement confirming that the fax was sent and received by the SSA office. The statement needs to be signed and dated by the clerk. Remember, due to the large volume of mail and faxes received by the SSA every day, many documents may become lost. Documents you send using other fax machines, and even if verified by the receiving SSA office, often fail to show up in your file -- they simply vanish!

You may find that many letters are written, but mailed late by the SSA. Keep all letters you receive from the SS and the envelopes as evidence.

If the date on the envelope is vastly different, more than 3 days, from the date on the letter itself, you need to file an Unfair Treatment Complaint.

With short response deadlines, every day is crucial. If you have only 30 days to reply, from the date on the letter, and if the letter was sent late this reduces your available response time. You could lose by default if you cannot complete you response reply and have your documents reach the SSA by the deadline.

If you have time, you can use snail mail, but always send it registered with a return receipt, dated, and signed by the receiver. Keep this receipt as it will be evidence that your requests, briefs and other documents were mailed and received by the SSA on the day stamped on the receipt.

Finally, call the receiving SSA office to double check that the documents were received and are in your file. Make a note of the clerk's name and time you called. Most cell phones will automatically save the phone number, date and time of every call. These records may be used as evidence if you are told the SSA never received a response from you.

Be careful and assume nothing. Your local SS office will not provide any fax numbers, so you must use the fax number in the letterhead you received from the SSA. If the fax number fails to accept your fax due to a "mail box full" message, call the SSA repeatedly, until you have a working fax number.

Unfavorable Decisions

If your decision is unfavorable, ask for a review by the *SSA Review Council* using *form HA-520*. This form only requires that you formally declare your request for a review, answer a few questions related to your case, and state the reason you believe the ALJ's decision was wrong. A second and different ALJ will review your case and issue a second decision.

You will need to submit this form within 60 days of receiving the decision letter from the first ALJ for your claim to remain active. The 60 days starts 5 days from the date on the letter inside – NOT on the envelope or when you actually received it.

> **Without submitting this form,**
> **your case will end**
> **with the first ALJ's decision.**

As these deadlines may change from time to time, always check the number of days you are given to submit your reply.

Don't be afraid to call the SSA to confirm

whether the deadline is

the date mailed or the

date they receive

your documents.

Favorable Decisions

If your case is favorable, or partially favorable, the Review Council will look at the judge's decision and may overturn it. You may appeal this ruling by filing a civil action with the district court in your state.

The former appeal steps are free, but the cost to file your case in District Court is quite reasonable if you represent yourself. In Colorado, it will cost you about $100. Your state should be similar.

The one benefit of going to court is that your appeal case will become a part of the judicial records and will add to the increasing number of cases regarding the SS offsets. Each case helps in the fight to get the offsets repealed.

District Court

You start your civil action by *filing a brief* in District Court. You may file your own brief and represent yourself as a "pro se" plaintiff. You should not hire an attorney, unless they are free, as their fees may outweigh any financial awards you may receive.

> *NOTE: "Pro se" is Latin meaning*
> *- "for oneself -- on one's own behalf."*
>
> www.law.cornell.edu/wex/pro_se

Taking the SSA to court should be your last resort. A judge cannot rewrite or amend the POMS laws, but they can be sure the offset regulations were correctly applied.

Representing Yourself

You will be amazed at how easy it is to represent yourself in court as a "pro se" plaintiff. If you call your state's District Court, they usually will provide you with information on how to write a brief and file your case. They will also furnish you with forms and instructions and from whom, if you are eligible, you may obtain free legal help. You will be given a lot of leeway in the writing format of your brief since you are not an attorney.

A good reference book is *"Federal Rules of Civil Procedure" Educational Edition, by West,* and you can usually find a used copy on Amazon. The cost for a used book runs about $20. The first pages are a must read as they describe step by step what you need to do when filing a civil action. The book is large, but you will be using only a very small portion, mainly Rule 4 and Rule 26. You may also use as a cross reference the internet site: **www.law.cornell.edu/rules/frcp/rule_4 or 26**

Writing A Brief
Never heard of or wrote a brief?

Don't be afraid. Appendix E has a sample brief as do many web sites.

One of the best sites is:

courts.oregon.gov/.../civilcasesampleacceptableappellants

Also -- **www.peoples-law.org/preparing-your-case-**

www.ninth.courts.state.oh.us/Information.htm
Guide to Brief Preparation."

The Sections and Layout of a Brief

Part 1:   Where you list each issue in detail.
>> Number each issue as 1, 2, 3 etc.

Part 2:   Where you explain why you object or believe the decision on each issue is wrong.
>> Refer to the number of the issue you are addressing.

Part 3:   Where you request how you want the judge to rule on each issue.   Again use the number of each issue and what decision you are requesting from the judge.

On the last page, you sign & date the brief; file it with the court, provide the Certificate of Service and, pay the fee.

The "*Certificate of Service*" is just a written and signed statement from you that on such and such a date you sent the required copies of your brief, by email or registered mail, to the SSA office and the SSA attorneys informing them that you have filed a civil action.

Appendix E has a sample of a Certificate of Service.

A sample of the Certificate of Service may also be found at:
www.tsc.state.tn.us/sites/default/files/docs/acc_certificate_of_service_o.PDF

Once your brief is filed, you will be expected to meet tight deadlines in submitting your reply arguments to the issues listed in the response brief filed by the SSA.

As soon as you receive a copy of the SSA brief immediately, send a request for a 30 to 60 day *extension of time*, EOT, to file your reply. Always do this immediately even if you think you do not need extra time.

The web site to file for an extension of time is:
www.ssa.gov/OP_Home/hallex/1-03-14.html

Aug. 4, 2015 – A claimant may request an extension of time (EOT) to submit additional evidence or arguments to the Appeals.....

U.S. Circuit Court of Appeals

If you have lost your case in District Court,
it's time to STOP.

Do not bother to appeal to the U.S. Court of Appeals for four reasons.

1. These courts seldom overturn a district court decision and will usually support the Commissioner's decision.

2. It is going to become very time consuming and expensive.

3. An Appeals Court cannot rewrite or change the POMS regulations. Only Congress and the President have the authority to amend and write laws. The Court only verifies that the regulations were correctly applied.
4

4. It is now time to go after your state agency regarding your right to reject the matching funds which trigger your offsets

How to File an Unfair Treatment Complaint

If you feel you are being treated unfairly by any of the SSA employees or judges, you may file an *Unfair Treatment Complaint.* And yes, there is a form for that too, called *SSA Publication No. 05-10071.*

The SSA provides the following guidelines on how to complain if you feel you were treated unjustly. Your complaint letter should include:

> *Your contact information, phone, email, local address*
>
> *Your Social Security number*
>
> *The name of the offending SSA employee*
>
> *Date when the incident occurred*
>
> *Name, phone number and address of any witnesses*

Your complaint should state your concerns as precisely as possible, making it clear the actions and words that you are objecting to, and what you considered to be unfair.

Mail your letter to: **The National Office of the SSA**
Office of Public Inquiries,
1100 West High Rise
6401 Security Blvd., Baltimore, MD 21235

Advocacy

When courts, government offices, or other organizations consider cases or policy decisions that affect consumers, the FTC may offer insight through "amicus briefs" or "advocacy letters." To learn how to write and effective advocacy letter go to: www.hlade.org/advocacy-letter.htm

If you don't succeed, it's time to take your complaints directly to your state pension agency, your Congressional Representatives in both the house and senate and directly to the President.

A sample letter and format is shown in Appendix D and you can find your *Representative contact information in Appendix B.*

It Only Takes One

Remember, it only takes one person to start the ball rolling. You could be another Candy Lightner, who organized MADD, Mothers Against Drunk Driving, after her 13-year-old-daughter was killed by a drunken driver in 1980.

Candy fought and won her battle to lower the DUI limits, to have tougher DUI laws, and to have roadside checkpoints. You or a loved one may be alive today because one person stood up and fought for change.

We can get these offsets repealed.

About Judge Lyle Douglas Olson

Judge Olson is an Administrative Law Judge in the Office of Hearings and Appeals for the SSA in Fargo, North Dakota. He graduated from the University of North Dakota's School of Law and was admitted to the Supreme Court October 6, 1987. ndcourts.gov/_court/lawyers/04527.htm

In 2015, Judge Olson disposed of 438 cases of which 240 were denied and 37 cases dismissed, leaving only 161 that actually were approved and granted a hearing.

In the U.S., in 2015, the cases requesting a hearing had on average a 37% denial rate, but for Judge Olson the denial rate was 55%. Judge Olson is a no-nonsense, by the book, demanding, strict, but fair, judge.

Reviewing over 400 cases every year for 28 years, Judge Olson knows the SS complex WEP and GPO offset regulations to the letter.

Judge Olson is a no-nonsense, by-the-book, demanding, strict but fair judge.

His decision, was six pages long and very detailed. In his written decision, Judge Olson methodically referenced the exact POMS regulation that pertained to each of the issues in my appeals case. Judge Olson stated that comparing the Lifetime Table to one's life expectancy would be:

like comparing apples to oranges, Judge Olson said, they are NOT one in the same.
Judge Olson also said offset penalties do end once the lump sum pension is depleted.

An appeals case does not receive a favorable decision from this Judge unless he finds it is a legitimate complaint backed by policies found in the POMS regulations.

I find it hard to believe that Judge Olson would be careless, misinterpret, or misunderstand any POMS regulation.

I find the SSA's accusation that he made an "*Error in Law*" as the reason they overturned his decision, to be preposterous and questionable.

Apples vs Oranges

The SSA Actuarial Department prepares statistics for both the lifetime of a lump sum and your life expectancy. Judge Olson wrote that the "Lifetime Table" is the "lifetime" of a sum of money-- not my life expectancy. SSA Judge Olson made this fact clear in his decision and wrote that you cannot substitute one table in place of another as they are not interchangeable.

Both of the tables may be found in Appendix E
or the SSA.gov web site under:
Life Expectancy Calculator and POMS RS 00605.364

These tables do not look the same because they are not.

Not So Fast, Replies the SSA

The SSA sent me a letter stating that Judge Olson's decision was incorrect, and the Commissioner was overturning Olson's decision. *Incredible!* The SSA stated that the *Lifetime Table of Actuarial Values* shown in the *POMS 605.364* regulation were the "life expectancies of a human being." The SSA also stated the offsets would never end but would be applied every month until the retiree died.

Why does *POMS RS 00605.360, C (5a)* say:
"*When WEP Application Ends*" -- if it never does?

Does anyone qualify for recomputation of their offsets?

Has anyone had their SS benefits fully restored?

SS offsets should never be applied if it means the retiree will live in poverty.

I wrote this book hoping it would help you become better informed and to better understand the POMS regulations, the unfair offsets and how your life expectancy is "modified. to: double or triple your monthly offset deductions.

I hope you will file an appeal; that you will spread the word to your colleagues and write to your Congressional Representatives requesting the offsets be repealed.

I thank you for buying this book and for taking your time to read it.

Sincerely,
Jeanette A. Wicks

Social Security Administration
www.socialsecurity.gov   410-965-0707

Contacting Members of Congress
thomas.loc.gov/home/contactingcongress.htmll

1. Members' individual Web sites provide comprehensive contact information:
   Senate Member Sites
   House of Representatives Member Sites

2. House "Write Your Representative" service

3. How to Contact U.S. Senators

4. The telephone for the U. S. Capitol Switchboard is 202-224-3121

U.S. Senators
www.senate.gov
To find a Bill number or mail addresses of senators
   http://index.about.com   *for quality information*

U.S. House of Representatives
www.house.gov 202-224-3121
Switchboard TTY 202-225-1904
Washington, DC   20515

This site gives links to find: Committees, Legislative Activity, Your State Representatives, Votes, Bills & Reports, Hearings, Archives, Library of Congress

White House
www.whitehouse.gov
Fax: 202-456-2461 .....Phone: 202-456-1111
1600 Pennsylvania Ave. N.W.
Washington, D.C. 20500

Connect with Government
www.usa.gov/contact   1-800-333-4636
blogs   Facebook   videos

Chair of Finance Subcommittee On Social Security, Pensions and Family Policy
www.finance.senate.gov   phone: 202-224-2315

"*Protecting SS and ensuring workers
receive the pensions they have earned.*"

713 Hart Senate Office Bldg.
Washington, DC 20510
Fax: 202-228-6321

Committee on Ways and Means
www.socialsecurity.gov/legislation/hearsings/
www.waysandmeans.house.gov   202-225-9263

NOTE*: the U.S. Capitol Police will refuse
sealed-package deliveries to ALL House office buildings.*
For questions please call 202-225-1721

Social Security Advisory Board
www.ssab.gov   202-475-7700
Email: SSAB@SSAB.gov   Fax: 202.475.7715
Snailmail: 400 Virginia Avenue, SW Suite 625
Washington, D.C. 20024

SSA Regional Offices

Contact regional program staff to <u>determine</u> if an
entity is included in and/or a position is
Covered by a State's section 218 agreement:

Atlanta Regional Office 404-562-1324

Alabama, Florida, Georgia, Kentucky, Mississippi,
North Carolina, South Carolina, Tennessee

Boston Regional Office 617-565-2895

Connecticut, Maine, Massachusetts, New Hampshire,
Rhode Island, Vermont

Chicago Regional Office 312-575-4239

Illinois, Indiana, Michigan, Minnesota, Ohio, Wisconsin

Dallas Regional Office 214-767-4224

Arkansas, Louisiana, New Mexico, Oklahoma, Texas

Denver Regional Office 303-844-5473

Colorado, Montana, North Dakota, South Dakota,
Utah, Wyoming

Kansas City Regional Office 816-936-5640

Iowa, Kansas, Missouri, Nebraska

New York Regional Office 212-264-1752

New Jersey, New York, Puerto Rico, Virgin Islands

Philadelphia Regional Office 215-597-1759

Delaware, DC, Maryland, Pennsylvania,
Virginia and West .Virginia

<u>San Francisco Regional Office</u> **888-829-0749**
American Samoa, Arizona, California, Guam, Hawaii,
Nevada, Saipan

<u>Seattle Regional Office</u> **206-615-2125**
Alaska, Idaho, Oregon, Washington

Legislative Interests at the Federal Level
retireesunited.org/pages/federal.html

visit **Contacting the Congress** page for directory
of addresses for the 540 members of the Congress.

Program Operations Manual System POMS
www.ssa.gov/policy *current regulations*

SS Trust Fund
www.treasury.gov/connect
Email: www.treasury.gov/connect/Pages/
Message-to-the-Secretary.aspx

U.S Department of Justice
www.justice.gov/oig   202-514-3435   800-869-4499

U.S. Department of Justice
Office of the Inspector General
950 Pennsylvania Avenue, N.W., Suite 4706
Washington, D.C. 20530-0001

Assistant Inspector General for Audit
www.oig.ssa.gov 1-800-269-0271 (10 - 4 EST)
Fax 410-597-0118

Social Security Fraud Hotline
P.O. Box 17785
Baltimore, Maryland 21
Links to reports, audits and investigations.
To report fraud, waste, or abuse or reduce improper
payments and increase overpayment recoveries

Federal Trade Commission Headquarters
202-326-2222   send mail to this address:
Federal Trade Commission
600 Pennsylvania Avenue, NW, Washington, DC 20580

For Individual Consumers
www.ftccomplaintassistant.gov
Complaints about fraud, scams, phishing, identity theft,
unwanted telemarketing, credit or debt issues, or other
unfair business practices may be submitted.

Office of Policy and Coordination 202-326-3300
Room CC-5422 Bureau of Competition
Federal Trade Commission
600 Pennsylvania Ave., NW , Washington, DC 20580

uspolitics.about.com
All federal officials have offices in their home districts as well
as an office in Washington, DC. A face-to-face meeting has
the potential to have more impact than a letter.

Office of Policy and Coordination
202-326-3300
Room CC-5422 Bureau of Competition
Federal Trade Commission 600 Pennsylvania Ave., NW
Washington, DC 20580

U.S. Government Printing Office
866-512-1800
Transcripts for Sale by the Superintendent of Documents,
     www.bookstore.gpo.gov

Must have H.R. or S Number and name
for example: H.R. 4391 or S. 2455 and name like:
" The "Public Servant Retirement Protection Act"
                         Or
Do a WEB search using same number and print your own.

Subcommittee on Social Security of the Committee on Ways and Means
www.gpo.gov/fdsys/pkg.CHRG
House of Representatives
U.S. Government Printing Office

Minutes of Hearing and a List of Organizations, Unions, State Teachers Organizations, Postal Workers, Fraternal Order of Police, National Treasury Employees Union and other groups and individuals presenting viewpoints at hearing.

May purchase documents from: U.S. Government Printing Office,
All Committee advisories and news releases are
available at: **www.waysandmeanshouse.gov**

Federal Digital System Gov't Publications
www.gpo.gov/fdsys   202-512-1800
Catalog of U.S. Government Publications
732 North Capitol Street, NW,
Washington, DC 20401-001

The Library of Congress
Law Library of Congress.gov

Guide to Law Online
General Information 202-707-5000
101 Independence Ave, SE
Washington, DC 20540

Social Security Fairness Act of 2015
H.R. 973 114th congress www.congress.gov
Get Alerts   Bill Information
Sponsor: Rep. Rodney Davis (R-Illinois)
www.kevinbrady.house.gov

WA Phone: 202-225-4901
TX Phone 936-441-5700 and 936-439-9532
301 Cannon House Office Building,
Washington, DC 20515

Find Co-Sponsors of Bills   www.thomas.loc.gov
Type in bill number in search box click on bill summary
and status, click on cosponsors

Government Tract
not affiliated with the Government

www.GovTrack.us/congress/bills
GovTract isn't affiliated with the government It is
funded solely from advertising.

This is one of the **world's most visited**
government transparency websites.
The site helps ordinary citizens find and track bills
in the U.S. Congress and understand their
representatives' legislative record.

How You Can Help
For more information contact mardito@retireeunited.org
Massachusetts Retirees United
314 Main Street   Unit 105,
Wilmington MA 01887

www.petition2congress.com/create
This petition is a fast and easy.
Just add your name along
with the   over 28,000 who have
already sent comments regarding WEP GPO offsets.

Government Agencies and Elected Officials
www.USA.gov is the U.S. government's official web portal
Services and Information 1-844-872-4681 *about*
USA.gov or about any government question you have.

Chat *Our web chat service is available Monday - Friday,*
8:00 AM until 8:00 PM Eastern
Our chat service is only available in English –
not available on federal holidays.

E-mail *your questions, suggestions, compliments, complaints, or technical problems about USA.gov or the government. We will respond (in English or Spanish) within two business days.*

Call us *at 1-844-872-4681 – Our information   specialists will answer your government questions   between 8:00 AM and 8:00 PM Eastern Time, Monday   through Friday, except federal holidays. This service is   available in English and Spanish. Recorded information   on frequently requested subjects is always available.*

Social Media   *You can connect with the government through   Facebook, Twitter, blogs, and more!*

Postal Mail

We prefer you <u>contact us by e-mail or phone</u>, so we can respond faster Our mailing address is:

U.S. General Services Administration
Office of Citizen Services and Innovative Technologies
1800 F Street, NW
Washington, DC 20405 U.S.A.

Windfall Elimination Program WEP
www.wep.gov

Government Pension Offset GPO
www.gpo.gov

Dual Entitlement
secure.ssa.gov/apps10/poms.nsf/lnx/0300615020

Life Expectancy Calculator
www.socialsecurity.gov/OACT/population/longevity

Social Security Publications
www.ssa.gov/pubs

Hallex
www.ssa.gov/hallex   www.wikipedia.org
Hearings, Appeals, Litigation Law

Court Case Decisions

www.ssa.gov/OP_Home/rulings/rulfind3.html

Cumulative Listing of Current Court Case Decisions

Published As Social Security Rulings 19960

Alaska

doa.alaska.gov/drb   Phone: 907-465-4460

Division of Retirement and Benefits   800-821-2251
6th Floor State Office Building   Fax: 907-465-3086
P.O. Box 110203, Juneau, AK 99811-0203

California

www.ca-retired-educator.blogspot.com :   916-228-5453
Email: Newsroom@Calstrs.com   916-923-2200

CA Retired Teachers Assoc. TRS (Calstrs)
800-228-5453
800 Howe Ave., Suite 370   Fax: 916-414-5040
P.O. Box 15275

Sacramento, CA 95851-0275   Phone: 916-444-3216
Association of CA School Admin.   800-608-2272
1029 J. Street, Suite 500   Fax: 916-444-3739
Sacramento, CA 95814

Colorado

www.copera.org   Phone: 800-759-7372
CO Public Employee's Retirement Assoc.
P.O. Box 5800,
1301 Pennsylvania St., Denver, CO 80203

P.O. Box 200
1120 West 122nd Ave., Westminster, CO 80020

Connecticut

www.cea.org

Connecticut Education Assoc.

Capitol Place, Suite 500

21 Oak Street, Hartford, CT 06106

hone: 860-525-5641

800-842-4316

Fax: 860-725-6323

Florida

www.dms.myflorida.com

Email:retirement@dms.myflorida.com

Florida Retirement System FRS

Local Retirement Section

Phone: 850-907-6500

850-907-6500

844-377-1888

Fax: 850-921-2161

Division of Retirement

1317 Winewood Blvd, Bldg 8

P.O. Box 9000,Tallahassee, FL 32315-9000

Police and Firefighters

Email: mph@dms.myflorida.com

Division of Retirement

P.O. Box 3010, Tallahassee, FL 32315-3010

Phone: 877-738-6737

850-922-0667

Georgia

www.ers.ga.gov

E-mail:human.resources@doc.k12.ga

Phone: 404-352-6500

: 404-352-6500

Employees' Retirement System of GA

ERS, JRS and LRA retirees

Two Northside 75, Suite 100

Atlanta, GA 30318

800-352-0650

Fax: 404-657-7840

Hawaii
ers.hawaii.gov/resources
Employees' Retirement System
City Financial Tower
201 Merchant St. Suite 1400
Honolulu, HI 96813-2980

Phone: 808-586-1735
Fax: 808-587-5766

Illinois
www.srs.illinois.gov
State Retirement Systems' of Illinois
160 N. LaSalle St., Suite S200, Chicago, IL 60601

Phone: 217-785-7019

Springfield, Illinois
2101 S. Veterans Parkway
P.O. Box 19255
Springfield, IL 62794-9255

Phone: 312-814-5853

Indiana
www.in.gov/inprs/2802.htm
ERM, PERF, TRF

Phone: 888-286-3544
Fax: 317-232-3882

Indiana Public Retirement System
One North Capital, Suite 100
Indianapolis, IN 46204

Kentucky
www.ktrs.ky.gov
E-mail: krs.mail@kyret.ky.gov
Kentucky Retirement Systems
1260 Louisville Road, Frankfort, KY 40601

Phone: 502-696-8800
       800-928-4646
Fax: 502-696-8822

Kentucky, con't

Teachers' Retirement System   Phone: 502-848-8500
www.mss.trs.ky.gov/PathwayMSS   800-618-1687
Email: ktrs.info@ky.gov   Fax: 502-573-0199
479 Versailles Road
Frankfort, KY 40601-3868

Louisiana

www.lrta.net   Phone: 225-927-8837
Email: info@lrta.net   888-531-1992
Louisiana Retired Teachers Assoc.   Fax: 225-927-8838
9412 Common St. Suite 5
Baton Rouge LA 70809

Maine

www.mainepers.org
Email: StateUnit@mainepers.org   Phone: 207-512-3100
Maine Public Emp. Retirement System   800-451-9800
280 Maine Avenue   Fax: 207-512-3101
Farmingdale, ME 04344
P.O. Box 349, Augusta, ME 04332-0349

Massachusetts

www.massretirees.com   Phone: 617-666-4446
Email: michael.williams@trb.state.ma.us   617-679-6880
Massachusetts Teachers' Retirement System
5 Middlesex Ave., Suite 304.
Somerville, MA 02145   Fax: 617-628-4002

Michigan

www.michigan.gov/ors Office
of Retirement Services P.O.
Box 30171
Lansing, MI 48909-7671

Phone: 517-322-5103
800-381-5111
Fax: 517-322-1116

Minnesota

www.msrs.state.mn.us/st-paul
Email: info@msrs.us

Minnesota State Retirement System
60 Empire Drive, Suite 300
St. Paul, MN 55103-3000

Phone: 651-296-2761
800-657-5757

Fax: 651-297-5238

Missouri

www.mnea..org
Missouri National Education Assoc .
PSRS PEERS MOSERS
1810 Elm Street
Jefferson City, MO 65101

Phone: 573-634-3202
800-392-0236
Fax: 573-634-5646

Montana

www.mpera.mt.gov
Email: mpera@mt.gov

Phone: 406-444-3154
877-275-7372
Fax: 406-444-5428

Public Employee Retirement Admin.
100 N Park Ave., Suite 200
P.O. Box 200131, Helena, MT 59620-0131

Nevada

www.nvpers.org

Nevada State Education Assoc.

693 W. Nye Lane

Carson City, NV 89703

Phone: 775-687-4200

866-473-7768

Fax : 775-687-5131

5820 S Eastern Ave., Suite 220

Las Vegas, NV 89119

Phone: 866-473-7768

Fax: 702-678-6934

New Hampshire

www.nhrs.org

Email: info@nhrs.org

New Hampshire Retirement System

54 Regional Drive, Concord, NH 03301-8507

Phone: 603-410-3671

877-600-0158

Fax: 603-410-3501

New Mexico

www.nmpera.org

Public Employees' Retirement Assoc.

Santa Fe Office

33 Plaza La Prensa, Santa Fe, NM 87507

Phone: 505-476-9300

800-342-3422

F ax: 505-476-9401

Albuquerque Office

2500 Louisiana Blvd. NE, Ste. 400

Albuquerque, NM 87110

Phone: 505-383-6550

Fax: 505-883-4573

New York

www.ose.state.ny.us/retire

New York State and Local

   Retirement System

110 State Street, Albany, NY 12244-0001

Phone: 518-474-7736

866-805-0990

Fax: 518-402-4433

Ohio

www.opers.org   Phone: 800-222-7377
Email: benefitquestions@opers.org   866-673-7748
Ohio Public Employee Retirement System
277 East Town Street   Fax: 860-725-6323
Columbus, OH 43215-4642

School Employees Retirement System SERS
300 East Broad St., Suite 100   phone: 614-222-5853
Columbus, OH 43215-3746   800-878-5853

Pennsylvania

www.ps.gov   Phone: 800-633-5461
Pennsylvania State Employees'   Fax: 717-237-0346
Retirement System
30 North 3rd St., Suite 150, Harrisburg, PA 17101

Rhode Island

www.ersri.org   Phone: 401-462-7600
Employees' Retirement System   Fax   401-462-7691
Of Rhode Island
ERSRI MERS BHDDH
50 Service Ave., Warwick, RI 02886

Tennessee

www.treasury.tn.gov   Phone: 800-922-7772
Email: TCRS.Member-Services@tn.gov
Tennessee Consolidated Retirement System
Tennessee Deferred Compensation Program
Andrew Jackson Bldg., 15th Floor
502 Deaderick Street, Nashville, TN 37243-0201

218 State Contacts ~ Appendix B

Texas

www.atpe.org   Phone: 800-777-2873

Email: info@atpe.org   Fax: 512-467-2203

Texas Assoc. of Public Employee Retirement Systems

TEXPERS   ATPE

305 E Huntland Dr., Suite 300

Austin, TX 78752

Washington

www.drs.wa.gov   Phone: 360-664-7000

State Dept. of Retirement Systems.

800-547-6657

6835 Capitol Blvd

Tumwater, WA 98501

Department of Retirement Systems

P.O. Box 48380

Olympia, WA 98504-8380

Wisconsin

www.swib.state.wi.us   Phone: 608-265-2257

Email: benefits@ohr.wisc.edu   608-263-4275

Wisconsin Retirement System   Fax: 608-265-1456

121 E. Wilson Street

P.O. Box 7842

Madison, WI 53707-7842

American Federation of State, County, and Municipal Employees, AFL-CIO

1625 L Street, NW   Washington, D.C. 20003

afscme.org

Approximately 3,400 local unions in 46 U.S. states, plus the District of Columbia and Puerto Rico.

The American Federation of State, County, and Municipal Employees (AFSCME) are the *largest trade union of public employees in the United States.* It represents approximately **1.4 million**[1] **public sector employees and retirees**, including health care workers, corrections officers, sanitation workers, police officers, firefighters,[3] and childcare providers.

Founded in Madison, Wisconsin in 1932, AFSCME is part of the AFL-CIO, one of the two main labor federations in the United States.

The union is known for its involvement in political campaigns, almost exclusively with the Democratic Party.[6] Major political issues for AFSCME include single-payer health care, protecting pension benefits, raising the minimum wage, preventing the privatization of government jobs, and extending unemployment benefits.

Postmasters of the United States

www.napus.org   40,000 Members

Phone: 703-683-9027   FAX 703-683-0923

8 Herbert Street, Alexandria, VA 22305

National Education Association NEA
https://en.wikipedia.org/wiki/National_Education_Association

Members: 2,963,121

Phone: 202-833-4000 ᴇᴛ   Fax: 202-822-7974
Mail: National Education Association
1201 16th Street, NW
Washington, DC 20036-3290
E-mail: educationvotes.nea.org/.../educators-fight-unfair-offsets

Use NEA's Activist Toolkit to fight
for GPO/WEP repeal

Labor Unions in the United States
en.wikipedia.org/wiki/

For a List_of_labor_unions_in_the_United_States

Unions exist to represent the interests of workers, who form the membership.

Under US labor law, the National Labor Relations Act 1935 is the primary statute which gives US unions rights. The rights of members are governed by the Labor Management Reporting and Disclosure Act 1959.

Grand Lodge Fraternal Order of Police
www.grandlodgefop.org   Phone: 800-451-2711
Represents **325,000** police officers.
ATNIP-ORMS Center   Phone 615-399-0900 CT
National Headquarters   FAX   615-399-0400
701 Marriott Drive,Nashville, TN 37214

Grand Lodge Fraternal Order of Police con't

The largest law enforcement labor organization in U.S.

National Legislative Office   Phone 202-547-8189

328 Massachusetts Ave. NE   FAX 202 547-8190

Washington, DC 20002   E-Mail:

legislative@fop.net

National Treasury Employees Union NTEU

www.nteu.org   Represents **150,000** employees

NTEU National Headquarters   Phone 202-572-5500

1750 H Street, NW,   202-572-5520

Washington, DC 20006

Representing federal employees NTEU is widely known as a smart, tough, and well-respected organization that is determined to represent employees before federal agencies, Congress and in the courts to protect and promote their rights.

National Active and Retired Federal Employees

Associations   NARFE   **350,000** Members

E-mail: hq@narfe.org   Phone: 703-838-7760 ET

www.narfe.org   Fax: 703-838-7785

NARFE Headquarters

606 N. Washington S, Alexandria, VA 22314-1914

Center for Retirement Research at Boston College

http://crr.bc.edu   e-mail: crr@bc.edu

Phone: 617-552-1762

Hovey House, 258 Hammond St.,Chestnut Hill MA 02467

Significant Reforms to State Retirement Systems
www.nasra.org

Retirement plan reforms focused on one of these goals, to the exclusion of others, are likely to produce **unintended negative outcomes.** Public pension reforms generally kept those core features known to balance retirement security.

AARP   www.aarp.org

Email: foundation@aarp.org   888-687-2277
Lisa Marsh Ryerson | *President, AARP Foundation*

Those who are 50, over, and struggling need a voice and an advocate now more than ever. AARP Foundation, a charitable affiliate of AARP, serves that purpose.

Building on AARP's reputation and expertise, AARP Foundation has the ability to support and work with local organizations and programs nationwide to coordinate, fill in the gaps, and help effective initiatives grow. This multiplier effect ensures we do not duplicate resources or reinvent the wheel.

By 2030, one in every five Americans will be age 65 or older. Let us not wait until poverty becomes a way of life they can never escape. Through the programs of AARP Foundation, we can give struggling Americans 50 and over a chance to recover their confidence, regain a foothold and stay on track. The more we do now, the less we will have to do later.

Older workers suffer the largest increase in long-term unemployment, the longest spells of joblessness, and the least likelihood of finding jobs. Many are living paycheck to paycheck, and one in four workers has burned through his or her savings. Having worked hard, paid taxes and served their country and communities, they find themselves in circumstances far beyond what they could have prepared for. Many of them are one-step short of economic catastrophe.

What many may not realize is that:

AARP has declined so far to take a stand on the repeal of the WEP and the GPO!

Please contact your congress people AND AARP
on this important issue and
**insist that they provide some very critical
support for these repeals.**

ProPublica

Investigative Reporting Journalism in The Public Interest
Phone: 1-212-514-5250   Fax: 1-212-785-2634
155 Avenue of the Americas,13th Floor ,
New York, N.Y. 10013

ProPublica was awarded the:
2011 Pulitzer Prize for National Reporting,
Two Emmy Awards in 2015 --
- Peabody Award in 2013

ProPublica was founded by Paul Steiger, the former managing editor of The **Wall Street Journal**. It is now led by Stephen Engelberg, a former managing editor of The Oregonian and former investigative editor of The **New York Times**, and Richard Tofel, the former assistant publisher of The Wall Street Journal.

We seek to <u>stimulate positive change</u>. We uncover unsavory practices in order to <u>stimulate reform</u>. We won't lobby. We won't ally with politicians or advocacy groups.

In areas ranging from product safety to securities fraud, from flaws in our system of criminal justice, institutions as unions, universities, hospitals, foundations and on the media when they constitute the **strong exploiting or oppressing the weak,** or when they are abusing the public **trust.**

By being persistent, by <u>shining a light on inappropriate practices continuing to do so until change comes about.</u>
In short, we stay with issues we strive to be fair.
We aggressively edit every story to assure
its accuracy and fairness.

Social Security Fairness
www.ssfairness.com   **E-mail:** ssfairness@gmail.com
Join mailing List and receive Latest Action Alerts, Survey's Answers frequently asked Questions about WEP and GPO

National Conference on Public Employee Retirement Systems The Voice for Public Pensions

Tel: 1-877-202-5706   Fax: 202-624-1439
444 N. Capitol St., NW Suite 630, Washington, D.C. 20001

More than 1,000 trustees, administrators, state and local officials, investment, financial and union officers, pension staff and regulators attend the yearly conference.

American Federation of Teachers AFL-CIO

www.aft.org   Phone 202-879-4400
555 New Jersey Ave. N.W.,
Washington DC 20001

Represents **1.3 million teachers** and other public servants nationwide State and Local Chapters: link and search by ZIP code

Help us get our message out to as many people as we can by liking us on Facebook, following us on Twitter.
Sign up for consumer alerts to stay in the loop
on the status of our battles and to
find out what you can do to help on a regular basis.

Massachusetts Retirees United

E-mail: contact@retireeunited.org
Phone: 781-365-0205   or 1-866-613-7360
Write: Massachusetts Retirees United
314 Main Street   Unit 105
Wilmington,   MA 01887

Legislative update on any retirement issue affecting both active and retired teachers of the Commonwealth of Massachusetts can be found here.

This site will enable you to reach any Senator or Representative on Beacon Hill. Simply click on their name.

SENATE: To find Massachusetts members of the Senate and

their phone click on: **https://malegislature.gov/people/senate**

HOUSE OF REPRESENTATIVES: To find Massachusetts members of the House and their phone click on:

http://retireesunited.org/pages/stateleg.html

Coalition to Preserve Retirement Security

112 S. Pitt St. Alexandria, VA 22314

TEL.: 703- 684-5236   FAX: 703-684-3417

The Coalition to Preserve Retirement Security (CPRS) is the leading voice and preeminent organization in Washington, D.C., dedicated to

**opposing efforts to force public employers
and their workers to participate
in the Social Security program.**

Our mission is to protect the current structure of public sector retirement plans. In addition, CPRS has advocated reform of the government pension offset **(GPO)** and the windfall elimination provision **(WEP),** which unfairly punish public employees covered by a public system who are also be entitled to Social Security benefits.

Coalition Organizations

narfewa.net/coalition_organizations

educationvotes.nea.org/.../educators-fight-unfair-offsets

NARFE has a number of Coalition Partners

The Fund to Assure an Independent Retirement (FAIR)

Today's member groups represent more than **six million** public service employees and retirees.

The 33 national federal and postal organizations

work to protect the economic and health

security of their members

The Coalition to Assure Retirement Equity (CARE)

Comprised of over 49 national, state, and local organizations solely for the

purpose of addressing the Social Security Offsets,

the Government Pension Offset (GPO)

and the Windfall Elimination Provision (WEP).

Like federal annuitants, many state and local government retirees are also affected by the GPO and WEP.

The Leadership Council of Aging Organizations (LCA

www.lcao.org
NARFE is an active member of LCAO, a coalition of 64 national nonprofit organizations concerned with the well-being of America's **older population.**

LCAO works on issues common to all **senior citizens**,

including **Medicare, Social Security**,

long-term care, and prescription drug costs.

The Military Coalition   www.themilitarycoalition.**org**

Today, NARFE and the 35 members of the Military Coalition, including the Military Officers Association of America (MOAA), promote premium conversion legislation; work on long-term care insurance, support pay parity.

The Coalition for Effective Change (CEC)

This is a non-partisan alliance of associations representing both active and retired federal managers, executives, and professionals. CEC seeks to provide a forum for these federal employees to assist in re-inventing government and to share their expertise with policymakers.

The Coalition for Effective Change brings together a diverse membership with a mission to improve government operations. Links to member organizations can also be found at

www.effective-change.org.

Retired Educators Coalition for SS Fairness
www.trta.org

Represents over **300,000 member**s in 15 states

Consumer Watchdog   www.consumerwatchdog.org

E-mail @ consumerwatchdog.org   Phone: 310-392-0522

Mail: 2701 Ocean Park Blvd., Suite 112

Santa Monica, CA 90405

Or D.C. Office: 413 E. Capitol St., SE, First Floor

Washington, D.C. 20003

Get involved: Every day of the year, **Consumer Watchdog's** advocates, attorneys, and organizers are fighting to hold corporations and politicians accountable.
Our power to make change depends on the involvement of real people.

Submit a Consumer Complaint

Over the years, consumer complaints have played a key role in our successful efforts to change laws and hold corporations accountable.

Please tell us your story

Connect With Us   Here is how you can help:

Help us get our message out to as many people as we can by liking us on Facebook, following us on Twitter and Pinterest, and downloading our free application on your iPhone or iPad.

Sign Up   www.consumerwatchdog.org

Sign up for consumer alerts to stay in the loop on the status of our battles and to find out what you can do to help on a regular basis

Learn How to Win

After 25 years of campaigns, we have figured out a thing or two about making grassroots action effective.

Also, pick up a copy of Consumer Watchdog President Jamie Court's new book, ***The Progressive's Guide to Raising Hell***, which tells the stories of many of our most historic victories.

*Check out our success stories where we discuss **how we win**, and use our methods to win your own battles.*

National Academy of Social Insurance

nasi@nasi.org   Twitter: @socialinsurance

Phone: 202-452-8097   Fax: 202-452-8111

1200 New Hampshire Avenue, NW   Suite 830

Washington, DC 20036 USA

This is a nonprofit, nonpartisan organization made up of the nation's leading experts on social insurance

Its mission is to advance solutions to challenges facing the nation by increasing public understanding of how social insurance contributes to economic security.

Mondo Times   www.mondotimes.com
Mondo Code LLC   720-565-8455 MT
P.O. Box 1288, Boulder, CO 80306

Search for newspapers, magazines, radio and TV stations and television networks - <u>over 33,000 media outlets</u> in 213 countries.

This is a massive site with all the top media contacts for newspapers, magazines, and radio and TV stations.

They will help you with Media Contact Information, links to MTV TV, PBS Public Broadcasting Service, ABC, NBC, CBS, USA Today, lifestyle: seniors, and much more.

*For example: the site will give you the **<u>top 100</u> <u>newspapers in the USA</u>** by <u>circulation</u>, their main <u>headquarters</u>, the owner their current <u>editor</u>, by name, for each paper*

*Just **<u>click on the link</u>** to any state you wish to view.*

Contact the editors of the top 100 USA ewspapers.
Email American newspaper editors from
<u>Easy Media List,</u>
www.easymedialist.com/usa/top100newspapers.html

And best of all - it's **<u>FREE</u>**.

However, they will design your own custom contact list.

Nations Magazine
www.TheNation.com
https://en.wikipedia.org/wiki/The_Nation
The Nation Company, L.P.,   212-209-5415
Newmark Holdings', 21st Floor
520 Eighth Ave,   New York City, NY 10018

> **The Nation** is the oldest continuously published
> weekly magazine in the United States, and the
> most widely read weekly journal of progressive political
> and cultural news, opinion and analysis.

The American Prospect www.pospect.org

The American Prospect is a quarterly American political magazine dedicated to American liberalism and progressivism.   Based in Washington, D.C., it's aim is to advance liberal and progressive goals through reporting, analysis and debate about today's realities and tomorrow's possibilities.

In 2014, the magazine re-purposed itself as a "quarterly journal of ideas." The magazine undertook a project to connect progressive organizations   through   its   **Moving   Ideas   Network www.movingideas.org**, where staff writes policy statements, advocacy actions, and reports. **The Prospect** was founded in 1990 by **Robert Kuttner, Robert Reich, and Paul Starr.**

Robert Kutter, Prof. Brandeis Univ. was interview by Tavis Smiley.
Shown on PBS Jan. 23, 2017 and is worth watching.
www.pbs.org/wnet/tavissmiley/professor/robert-kuttner

JACOBIN -- Editor & Publisher Bhaskar Sunkara
www.jacobinmag.com
Jacobin is a leading voice of the American left, offering socialist perspectives on politics, economics, and culture. The print magazine is released quarterly and reaches over
**25,000 subscribers, in addition to
a web audience of 1,000,000 a month**.

Top 50 Online Newspapers

www.onlinenewspapers.com/Top50/Top50-CurrentUS.htm

The New York Times (New York
Greenwich News Connecticut,

Daily News (New York, New York

Washington Post (Washington DC

New York Post (New York

Bessemer News (Alabama

USA Today (National, Arlington, Virginia

Los Angeles Times (California,)

Sussex County News (Delaware, Georgetown)

Colleton County News (South Carolina, Smoaks)

The Washington Times (Washington DC)

Blount County News (Alabama)

Wall Street Journal (New York)

Sylacauga News (Alabama,)

Chicago Tribune (Illinois)

Boston Herald (Massachusetts)

Charleston News (South Carolina,)

Charlotte Observer Online (North Carolina,)

Arizona Republic (Phoenix)

The Miami Herald (Florida)

Atlanta Journal-Constitution (Georgia)

The Boston Globe (Massachusetts)

The Dallas Morning News (Texas)

Hale County News (Alabama, Greensboro)

Houston Chronicle (Texas)

Books

Social Security Works
by Nancy J. Altman and Eric R. Kingson
www.SocialSecurityWorks.org

This book explains why **Social Security is NOT going broke**, yet we are being given political rhetoric distorting the facts from politicians hoping to win favor with (younger) voters. Extensively researched, the statistical facts and charts were provided and r**eviewed by Stephen C. Goss,** former chief Actuary of the Social Security Administration and the Deputy Chief Actuary, Alice H. Wake.

Why and how Social Security <u>should be expanded</u>, the writers give compelling analysis as to why this is not only possible but necessary, especially for our seniors.

*This is one of the best books written on Social Security – **a must read!***

Get What's Your's
by: Lawrence Kotlikoff www.getwhatsyours.org

This book explains how you can **maximize your benefits** and avoid making disastrous mistakes. Why applying for benefits early **can hurt you later on** and yet if you are married there is a way to have your cake and eat it too.

Learn how to use the legal strategies to make the most of your lifetime Social Security benefit.

Easy reading. No complicated techniques.
<u>Written for the lay person</u> with little knowledge
of the Social Security system.

Boston University economist Larry Kotlikoff has spent every week, for over three years, answering questions about your Social Security benefits

If you haven't yet read Larry's comprehensive coverage of the changing Social Security rules, check out <u>his columns</u>:

<u>"This is not how you fix Social Security"</u> and <u>"Congress is pulling the rug out from people's retirement decisions."</u>

Inequality For All   by Robert B. Reich
www.robertreich.org   Blog: www.robertreich.org
Twitter: rbreich / Facebook Robert Reich

Robert served as Secretary of Labor in the Clinton administration, for which Time Magazine named him one of the ten most effective cabinet secretaries of the twentieth century.

His film **Inequality for All** is now available
on DVD, Blu-ray and Netflix.

Other best sellers "**Aftershock**, "**The Work of Nations**,"
Beyond Outrage," and, his most recent,
"**Saving Capitalism**."

Other Books:

Social Security, Medicare & Government Pensions
21st Edition by Attorney Joseph Matthews

Social Security for Dummies 2015
2nd Edition by Jonathan Peterson AARP Executive

SS 101 A Crash Course in Government Benefits
by Alfred Mill

Grappling With Government Abuse
One Teacher's Journal --
My Social Security Nightmare
By Winifred N. Tappan 970-275-7366
www.ssa-oneteachersnightmare.com
Email: wint@2026gmail.com

Letter Format and Writing Tips

Today's Date
The Honorable (name-U.S. Senator)
United States Senate
Washington, D.C. 20510

or

The Honorable (name-U.S. Rep.)
U.S. House of Representatives
Washington, D.C. 20515

Dear Senator or Representative (Insert Last Name):

The first paragraph should be a short introduction of who you are and   what   bill (number   S#xxx or HR#xxx) you are requesting they cosponsor.

A brief explanation of the issue you are writing about.
How the WEP and/or GPO is impacting you.
Conclude by thanking them for their time and consideration.

Ask to be sent a written response to your letter and to
be kept on a mailing list regarding this issue.

Limit your letter to ONE page.

Mail or E-mail to addresses above.

Sample Letter

Dear Senator/Congressman:

I am a retired public educator from (insert where you taught) writing about two unjust Social Security provisions that affect hundreds of thousands of retired educators and other public employees across the country. These provisions are known as *the Government Pension Offset (GPO) and the Windfall Elimination Provision (WEP)._*I urge Congress to enact legislation repealing these two Social Security provisions.

The Government Pension Offset (GPO) eliminates or reduces the spousal benefit by two-thirds the value of a teacher's retirement benefit. The WEP reduces, but does not eliminate, a portion of an individual's Social Security earned from other work outside of his/her public employment.

I am affected by the (insert your personal story here about how the GPO, the WEP or both have affected you).

U.S. Senator _____ has introduced S.____, and U.S. Representative _____ has introduced H.R.#-_____that calls for complete repeal of both the GPO and WEP. I am asking that you support this legislation and to repeal GPO and WEP.

The repeal of the GPO and the WEP would greatly benefit thousands of public servants now being penalized for their life's work.

Lawmakers have promised to help seniors with various programs or reforms.

These are hard times for seniors living on fixed incomes. The costs of health insurance, prescription drugs, and general cost of living expenses continue to increase.

Sign_____

Date_____

NOTE: The authors and **bill numbers will change** with each session of Congress and should be obtained from the web site: Coalition to Preserve Retirement Security

narfewa.net/coalition
112 S. Pitt St.
Alexandria, VA 22314

TEL.: 703- 684-5236   FAX: 703-684-3417

POMS RS 00605.364
Effective Dates: 07/08/2016 - Present
Determining Pension Applicability, Eligibility Date, and Monthly Amount

A. Determining if payments are a pension

1. Pension contains employee and employer contributions

   a. If employer contributions or employer and employee contributions are used to determine the payment, it is generally a pension subject to the windfall elimination provision (WEP).

   b. If only employee contributions are involved and the payment amount is based on employee contributions plus interest, i.e., a savings plan, it is subject to WEP, only if it is the primary retirement plan.

2. **Withdrawals**

   a. Withdrawals of the employee's own contributions and interest made before the employee is eligible to receive a pension are not pensions for WEP purposes if the employee forfeits all rights to the pension. This rule applies even if the employer paid the employee contributions.

   b. Withdrawals of the employee's own contributions and interest made after the employee is eligible to receive a pension are considered a lump-sum pension for WEP purposes.

   c. Any separation payment, withdrawal, or refund consisting of both employer and employee contributions is a pension; for WEP purposes

    d. whether made before or after the employee is eligible to receive a pension.

3. Payment from primary retirement plans and optional savings plans

    a. Payments received from defined contribution plans (e.g., 401(k), 403(b), or 457 plans) based on non-covered employment are considered a pension subject to WEP regardless of the source of contributions (employer only, employee only, or a combination of both), if the plan is the primary retirement plan. If the plan is a supplemental plan, the payments are subject to WEP when the plan payments contain employer or both employer and employee contributions.

    b. Payments from optional savings plans (e.g., the Federal Thrift Savings Plan for Civil Service Retirement System (CSRS) employees) are not considered a pension for WEP. For payments to qualify for this exclusion, the savings plan must be separate from the retirement plan and yield only the amount the employee paid in (plus interest and dividends), rather than an amount calculated based upon certain conditions such as age, earnings, and length of service.

    c. Pension payments that include voluntary employee contributions, that are separate, and in addition to, the regular pension payment are not subject to WEP.

4. Pensions that include payment based on another individual's earnings

    a. When a pension is based on the work and earnings of another individual in addition to the work and earnings of the number holder (NH), consider only

b. that portion of the pension attributable to the NH's non-covered earnings for WEP.

c. Prorate the pension to determine the portion of the pension based on the NH's non-covered earnings. Use the pension-paying agency's measuring methods (credits, months, etc.) to define the proration factors.

d. For pensions with partial non-covered situations, use WEP guarantee procedures RS 00605.370B.2. The numerator is the NH's non-covered service and the denominator is the total service.

B. Determining eligibility date

1. Date first eligible

a. An individual becomes eligible for a monthly pension or a lump sum in lieu of a monthly pension the first month he or she meets all requirements for payment except stopping work and applying for the payment.

b. The pension-paying agency, not SSA, determines pension eligibility and entitlement. Some defined benefit plans and defined contribution plans have specific requirements an individual must satisfy to be considered eligible for or entitled to a pension payout (i.e., periodic or lump sum payment). Review the plan's requirements to determine whether to apply WEP. See appropriate regional issuances for guidance on specific defined contribution plans.

c. Service credits that the worker purchased for the plan are included in determining the pension eligibility date regardless of when the worker purchased service credits. This includes credits for military service for a Federal pension even if the employee did not waive the military pension. (For proofs required, see RS 00605.366.)

2. Employment or vesting before 1986

Employment in a company or vesting in its pension plan before 1986 in itself does not constitute pension eligibility. The worker must have been eligible to receive a retirement or disability pension payment (either monthly or lump sum) from the pension plan before 1986 for the WEP exemption to apply.

C. Determining the monthly pension amount

1. Monthly payments

To apply the WEP guarantee, determine the gross monthly pension amount payable before reduction for:

- health insurance,
- survivor annuities,
- allotments,
- assignment of pensions (e.g., spouse's share of pension), and
- reduction in monthly pension amount because of contribution withdrawal by the worker.

Note: If an individual is entitled to a prorated pension amount in the first month of concurrent entitlement because of a mid-month entitlement to the pension, use the full monthly gross pension amount.

2. Payments paid on other than a monthly basis

Allocate payments made on "other than a monthly basis" on a basis equivalent to a monthly payment. Determine the amount the worker would have received if the pension were paid on a monthly basis by:

- a. multiplying a weekly pension amount by 52 and then dividing by 12; or

86r00-2260.

   b. multiplying a bi-weekly pension amount by 26 and then dividing by 12; or

   c. dividing annual or semi-annual pension payments by 12 or 6 respectively.

Use the equivalent monthly pension amount in determining the WEP guarantee. Use the month for which the partial payment was made as the first month of concurrent entitlement; however, we still use the equivalent pension rate to determine the WEP guarantee since the statute requires the guarantee be determined only with the month of first concurrent entitlement to the pension and RIB or DIB.

3. Multiple pensions

If the claimant is entitled to more than one pension that meets the criteria for WEP, consider each pension independently. To apply WEP the monthly amount is equal to the sum of the applicable monthly pensions.

4. Unique payments

When an employer or pension-paying agency allows an individual who is eligible for retirement or disability benefits to determine the disbursement amount, the duration of the pension or the start date, WEP is applicable when the individual first becomes entitled to the pension per RS 00605.360B.3. Treat the pension as a lump sum and follow the instructions in the next subsection RS 00605.364C.5.

5. Entire pension paid in a lump sum

When the entire pension is paid in a lump sum, the amount may represent a payment for a specific period of time or a "lifetime." Generally, the pension-paying agency will prorate the lump sum to determine a monthly amount for WEP purposes.

If the agency will not provide this information, prorate the lump sum to determine the monthly pension amount as follows:

a. Specific Period - Divide the lump sum by the number of months in the period specified by the pension-paying agency. See RS 00605.360C.5.a. for when WEP application ends.

b. Lifetime or Unspecified Period - Divide the pension lump sum amount by the appropriate actuarial value in the table that corresponds to the worker's age on the date of the lump sum award.

Table of Actuarial Values in Months				
Age on the Lump Sum Award Date	Lump Sum Award Date 6/1/2016 or later	Lump Sum Award Date 6/1/2011 through 05/31/2016	Lump Sum Award Date 6/1/2007 through 05/31/2011	Lump Sum Award Date 5/31/2007 or Earlier
40 or under	278.1	183.1	179.7	172.7
41	274.5	181.7	178.3	171.1
42	270.7	180.2	176.8	169.3

Table of Actuarial Values in Months

Age on the Lump Sum Award Date	Lump Sum Award Date 6/1/2016 or later	Lump Sum Award Date 6/1/2011 through 05/31/2016	Lump Sum Award Date 6/1/2007 through 05/31/2011	Lump Sum Award Date 5/31/2007 or Earlier
43	266.9	178.6	175.2	167.6
44	263.1	177.1	173.6	165.7
45	259.2	175.4	172.0	163.8
46	255.2	173.7	170.2	161.8
47	251.1	171.9	168.4	159.7
55	216.8	155.6	151.5	140.9
56	212.3	153.2	149.0	138.3
57	207.7	150.7	146.5	135.6
58	203.0	148.2	143.9	132.8
59	198.3	145.5	141.2	130.0

Table of Actuarial Values in Months

Age on the Lump Sum Award Date	Lump Sum Award Date 6/1/2016 or later	Lump Sum Award Date 6/1/2011 through 05/31/2016	Lump Sum Award Date 6/1/2007 through 05/31/2011	Lump Sum Award Date 5/31/2007 or Earlier
60	193.5	142.8	138.4	127.2
61	188.6	140.1	135.6	124.2
62	183.6	137.3	132.8	121.3
63	178.6	134.4	129.8	118.2
64	173.5	131.4	126.8	115.2
65	168.4	128.4	123.8	112.1
66	163.2	125.3	120.7	109.1
67	158.0	122.1	117.5	106.0
68	152.8	118.8	114.4	102.9
69	147.6	115.5	111.1	99.8

Table of Actuarial Values in Months

Age on the Lump Sum Award Date	Lump Sum Award Date 6/1/2016 or later	Lump Sum Award Date 6/1/2011 through 05/31/2016	Lump Sum Award Date 6/1/2007 through 05/31/2011	Lump Sum Award Date 5/31/2007 or Earlier
70	142.4	112.2	107.8	96.7
71	137.1	108.7	104.5	93.5
72	131.9	105.3	101.2	90.4
73	126.7	101.8	97.8	87.2
74	121.5	98.3	94.4	84.0
75	116.3	94.8	91.0	80.9
76	111.1	91.2	87.5	77.7
77	106.0	87.6	84.0	74.6
78	101.0	84.0	80.5	71.6
79	96.0	80.4	77.1	68.6

6. Federal pension

When a pension is based on both Federal Employees' Retirement System and CSRS service, it is treated as one pension. Because the pension is based on both covered and non-covered service, consider only the portion of the pension for the period of non-covered service in applying WEP. To prorate the pension, see RS 00605.370B.2.

D. Change in pension amount

A change in the amount of the beneficiary's pension or entitlement to additional pensions will not affect the initial primary insurance amount (PIA) determined under WEP. However, if the pension ceases and the NH is no longer entitled to the pension, recompute the PIA without considering the pension effective with the first month for which the claimant is no longer entitled to the pension. Entitlement to the pension does not cease if the NH voluntarily stops receiving benefits for a period of time and resumes them at a later date. In situations where NH has control over disbursement, see **RS 00605.364C.4. in this section.**

SSA - POMS: RS 00605.360 - -

06/24/2013
a newer version was not available (May 2017)

5. When WEP application ends

The WEP computation is no longer used when:

a. <u>the entitlement to the pension payment ceases or the proration of a lump sum payment based on a specified period ends,</u>

b. the NH dies (in the month of the NH's death, the PIA is recalculated without applying WEP), or

d. the NH becomes eligible for the WEP exemption by earning 30 YOCs. (The system will automatically identify additional YOCs and consider a recomputation for WEP.)

Table of Actuarial Values in Months

Age on the Lump Sum Award Date (years)	Actuarial Value Lump Sum Award Date 6/1/2016 or later	Actuarial Value Lump Sum Award Date 6/1/2011 through 05/31/2016	Actuarial Value Lump Sum Award Date 6/1/2007 through 05/31/2011	Actuarial Value Lump Sum Award Date 5/31/2007 or Earlier
48	247.1	170.1	166.6	157.6
49	242.9	168.2	164.7	155.4
50	238.7	166.3	162.7	153.2
51	234.4	164.3	160.6	150.8
52	230.1	162.2	158.4	148.4
53	225.8	160.1	156.2	146.0
54	221.3	157.9	153.9	143.5
55	216.8	155.6	151.5	140.9
56	212.3	153.2	149.0	138.3
57	207.7	150.7	146.5	135.6
58	203.0	148.2	143.9	132.8
59	198.3	145.5	141.2	130.0
60	193.5	142.8	138.4	127.2
61	188.6	140.1	135.6	124.2

Table of Actuarial Values in Months

Age on the Lump Sum Award Date (years)	Actuarial Value Lump Sum Award Date 6/1/2016 or later	Actuarial Value Lump Sum Award Date 6/1/2011 through 05/31/2016	Actuarial Value Lump Sum Award Date 6/1/2007 through 05/31/2011	Actuarial Value Lump Sum Award Date 5/31/2007 or Earlier
62	183.6	137.3	132.8	121.3
63	178.6	134.4	129.8	118.2
64	173.5	131.4	126.8	115.2
65	168.4	128.4	123.8	112.1
66	163.2	125.3	120.7	109.1
67	158.0	122.1	117.5	106.0
68	152.8	118.8	114.4	102.9
69	147.6	115.5	111.1	99.8
70	142.4	112.2	107.8	96.7
71	137.1	108.7	104.5	93.5
72	131.9	105.3	101.2	90.4
73	126.7	101.8	97.8	87.2
74	121.5	98.3	94.4	84.0

Table of Actuarial Values in Months

Age on the Lump Sum Award Date (years)	Actuarial Value Lump Sum Award Date 6/1/2016 or later	Actuarial Value Lump Sum Award Date 6/1/2011 through 05/31/2016	Actuarial Value Lump Sum Award Date 6/1/2007 through 05/31/2011	Actuarial Value Lump Sum Award Date 5/31/2007 or Earlier
75	116.3	94.8	91.0	80.9
76	111.1	91.2	87.5	77.7
77	106.0	87.6	84.0	74.6

6. Federal pension

When a pension is based on both Federal Employees' Retirement System and CSRS service, it is treated as one pension. Because the pension is based on both covered and non-covered service, consider only the portion of the pension for the period of non-covered service in applying WEP. To prorate the pension, see RS 00605.370B.2.

A change in the amount of the beneficiary's pension or entitlement to additional pensions will not affect the initial primary insurance amount (PIA) determined under WEP.

However, if the pension ceases and the NH is no longer entitled to the pension, recompute the PIA without considering the pension effective with the first month for which the claimant is no longer entitled to the pension.

Entitlement to the pension does not cease if the NH voluntarily stops receiving benefits for a period of time and resumes them at a later date. In situations where NH has control over disbursement, see RS 00605.364C.4. in this section.

Actuarial Life Table
Office of the Chief Actuary
https://www.ssa.gov/oact/STATS/table4c6.html

A period life table is based on the mortality experience of a population during a relatively short period of time. Here we present the 2011 period life table for the Social Security area population. For this table, the period life expectancy at a given age is the average remaining number of years expected prior to death for a person at that exact age, born on January 1, using the mortality rates for 2011 over the course of his or her remaining life.

The table is as close to the LE of those who have retired between 2000 to 2010.

Life Table 2011 in Years

Age	Male	Female		Age	Male	Female
55	25.38	28.67		69	14.81	17.09
56	24.57	27.8		70	14.13	16.33
57	23.78	26.93		71	13.47	15.59
58	22.99	26.07		80	8.13	9.58
59	22.21	25.22		81	7.62	9
60	21.44	24.37		82	7.14	8.43
61	20.67	23.52		83	6.68	7.89
62	19.9	22.68		84	6.23	7.37
63	19.15	21.85		85	5.81	6.87
64	18.4	21.03		86	5.4	6.4
65	17.66	20.22		87	5.02	5.94
66	16.93	19.42		88	4.65	5.52
67	16.21	18.63		89	4.31	5.12
68	15.51	17.85		90	4	4.75

Sample Brief

IN THE UNITED STATES DISTRICT COURT
FOR THE DISTRICT OF COLORADO
Judge YOUR JUDGE'S NAME

YOUR NAME v. Social Security Administration

Civil Action No **Your case number**

TYPE YOUR NAME, Pro Se

Plaintiff

v.

Name (of current Commissioner,) Commissioner of Social Security

Defendant

PLAINTIFF'S (you) REPLY BRIEF

APPEARANCES:
For Defendant:
JOHN F. WALSH, United States Attorney

J. BENEDICT GARCIA, Chief, Civil Division
United States Attorney's Office
District of Colorado
J.B.garcia@usdoj.gov

SANDRA T. KRIDER
Special Assistant United States Attorney
Supervisory Attorney
Office of the General Counsel
Social Security Administration
1001 17 Street
Denver, Colorado 80202
(303)844-0015
sandra.krider@ssa.gov

Attorneys for the defendant

Of counsel:
John Jay Lee
Regional Chief Counsel
Social Security Administration

TABLE OF CONTENTS REPLY BRIEF

STATEMENT OF JURISDICTION   1

STATEMENT NEW ISSUES   2-5

ARGUMENTS   5-15

CONCLUSION   16

NEW EXHIBITS UMBER   34, 35, 36, 37, 38, 39, 40

STATEMENT OF JURISDICTION

This Court has jurisdiction to review a final decision of the Commissioner under the Act. 42 U.S.C. 405 (g)

STATEMENT OF THE ISSUES

1. Defendant's Response Brief submitted to the Court on January XX, 20XX.

2. OBJECTIONS - In section two I will list my objections to what I feel are vague opinions not supported by evidence, material documents nor POMS regulations.

3. Definition of the word "EQUAL" and how it impacts the offsets.

4. Authority limitations of the Commissioner of Social Security

SECTION ONE - ERRORS IN (SSA) DEFENDANT'S BRIEF

---

1. <u>Exhibit 17</u> - the statement "No comments or additional evidence have been received." This is now being contradicted in the Defendants brief. In the Defendant's brief we find these conflicting statements.

   LIST THE EXHIBITS, PAGE # AND ISSUE

   First the Appeals Council stated "no comments received", now we find they reverse this and restate they were "received but not in the record."

   Are they now creating a new story to add facts?

2. <u>Exhibit 31</u>   28 USC 2412 - Costs and fees. This statue is explicit. Yet the brief states they made an error. How can all these attorney's make such a simple error? One has to question their competency.

   <u>Page 17   footnote #9</u>   "recognized this was an error" in stating I was NOT entitled to my costs and expenses should I be the prevailing party.

3. <u>Exhibits 2 and 4</u>   Misunderstanding of the Modified Lifetime Chart. This chart has headings which indicate that this is a "Table of Actuarial Values" The chart clearly indicates "*Actuarial Value Lump Sum Award*"

   The lifetime rule and corresponding Actuarial Value Lump Sum Award Table gives the specific time period (in months) that a lump sum is to be prorated

   This chart also determines the dollar amount of the offset for each month. It is found by dividing the lump-sum by the number of months listed beside the worker's age at the time the lump sum was awarded.

   <u>Exhibit 4   p. 3</u>   Divide the pension lump sum amount by the appropriate actuarial value in the table below that corresponds to the worker's age on the date of the lump sum award.

   <u>Exhibit 4 p. 2   #3</u>   ......"*prorate* the lump sum as follows" This statement clearly states the sum is to be prorated. The word "lifetime" is repeatedly used interchangeably with the word "pension".

   The numbers in the Lifetime Chart represent the number of months for which the sum is to be prorated.

At the end of the prorated period the pension ceases to
exist and the claimants PIA (primary insurance amount)
is to be recomputed without consideration of the pension.

Page 4 of Defendants Brief   The ALJ concluded that
the lump sums were to be *prorated* over a specified number
of months, after which the lump sums were "extinguished" and
the WEP and GPO would no longer apply (tr.25-26)

If the pension were based upon my life expectancy than we would be using
the Life Expectancy Tables (shown in Exhibit 21) for an individual.

The offset would be calculated 31.7 years x 12 = 380.40 months.

The Lump Sum would then be prorated as $22,144.08 / 380.40 which gives
us $58.21 x2/3 or a $38.80 offset per month and not the current $157.16

3.   The SS attorney's are substituting words into the POMS that are
     not in the official POMS documents. They appear to be trying
     to change the intended meaning of the POMS regulations.

This then can influence another's perception of the true facts. Thus the
defense brief may divert or sway the courts view and possibility lead
the judge (court) to concur with their (defendant) faulty conclusions,
their faulty logic and fabricated facts.

Below are some of the defendant's statements:

Page 11 of the defendants' brief states: ..."must be prorated over *Plaintiff's*
lifetime, i.e. for as long as she remains entitled to survivor's benefits."

This conclusion is in *error.*   No where in the POMS regulations is the word
"Plaintiff" nor the statement "*as long as she is entitled*" used.

Page 13 of the defendants' brief states :   ....."sum must be prorated as though received
monthly over the *individuals* lifetime."

POMS GN 02608.400 (A) *Exhibit 4 does not* have this wording anywhere in
its official document. It *does not* use the word "individual" before lifetime.

Exhibit 17 Again the defendant inserts the word "*claimant's* " before the word
lifetime. The defendant has no legal authority to rewrite the official POMS
documents.

It appears that they (the defendants) feel that if they can't win by telling or
showing the truthful facts, they can just make up something to conform to t
heir position.

Exhibit 23 - SS brochure Under the heading "some exceptions"
the SS brochure states:

"The Windfall Elimination Provision *does not apply* to survivors benefits"

Page 5 At the bottom of page 5, the defendants use the graph's hypothetical
example and states:

"if the WEP reduced Plaintiff's retirement benefit, her survivor's
benefit would increase by a corresponding amount."

If's - I will not waste the court's valuable time in addressing this "if"
nor the endless "if possibilities" the defendants can contrive.

This is a meaningless graph. This graph only demonstrates
two things:

1. The attorneys can add and subtract.
2. They do not understand the WEP GPO regulations
   nor how, when or which one of the POMS offset
   regulations applies.

The PIA (primary insurance account) is what determines whether
one applies WEP or GPO.

When I receive benefits on "my own earnings" we apply WEP regulations.
PIA is my own account and is under WEP .

When I applied for survivor's spousal benefits, the WEP drops out of the
equation. The SS survivor's benefit will now be based "on the earnings
of the deceased spouse" PIA is now that of the deceased husband and
GPO applies.

4. The power of the Commissioner

One must question the motive, creditability and competency of these attorneys
when so many errors are found in their brief..
In most cases they have failed to support their statements with documents.

CONCLUSION

Due to the overwhelming evidence presented in favor of the plaintiff I submit that the WEP/GPO offsets, prorated for the two lump sums, in fact do have ending dates.

For the foregoing reasons, the decision of the Appeals Council should be reversed. My PIA SS benefits be recalculated as of June 2009 and I be 100% reimbursed for the wrongfully deducted offsets plus interest.

That the current and all future offsets be recomputed without consideration of the first pension of $22,...41. That the second pension of $4,.....09 be considered expired on October 29, 2015.

At that time my offsets should cease and recomputation of my PIA SS benefits at that time would not consider either PERA pensions.

I am also requesting compensation for all my costs and expenses since June 2009 connected to fighting these issues.

I am requesting punitive damages due to stress from the inconsistencies in the decisions of the many SSA judges and staff.

Respectfully submitted this 4th day of February, 2013

Type YOUR NAME, Pro Se

> *Your name, Pro Se*
> Your mailing Address
>
> *Cell Phone:*
> Home Phone:
>
> Sign your name:_____
> Date:_____

A

Advocacy

briefs, amicus	196
email campaign	160
letter, advocacy	196
letter, how to write	196
MADD - Organizer	196
only takes one	196
www.hlade.org / advo	196

Age

encourage seniors to retire	171
full retirement age in 2017	23
increasing retirement age	122
lower full retirement age	171

Administrative Law Judge

ALJ hearing by	187
ALJ is independent	188
ALJ Lyle Olson	83
ALJ written decision	188
CD / written transcript	188
favorable decision	188
hearing denied	187
hearing form HA 501-U5	187
POMS RS605.364 ref	83
to keep claim active	190
written list of questions	187

Annuities

annuity is insurance	178
anti-competitive conduct	147
die within a certain period	178
insurance - annuities	73
lifetime payments	100
orig investment, owned by	100
unused monthly payments	178

Antitrust Laws

acting unreasonably	144
antitrust laws	140
attempt to monopolize trade	143
bad faith / misrepresenting	144
bottlenecks to competition	139
breach of contract	144
cheating people of money	142
Clayton Act	142
Clayton Section 7	142
collusion	140
competition reduced	140
competition closed	139
competition harmed	141
competition increased	139
competition promoted	140
competition unfair methods	143
conspiracy	141
Consumer Protection Bur.	142
Council Economic Adv.	140
deceptive acts or practices	141
dominant position	143
exclusionary contracts	143
Federal Trade Commission	141
fraud investigations	142
FTC insight	196
good faith and fair dealing	144
horizontal conduct	143
horizontal limits competition	143
horizontal may be illegal	144
injurious to consumers	141
insurance contract breach	144
leveling the playing field	140
McCarran 15 USC§1011-1015	145
McCarran-Ferguson Act	145
mergers and acquisitions	142
monopolization	141
monopoly created	142
not acting independently	143
policy decisions/consumers	196

price fixing, rigged bids	144
prices high	143
refusal to pay claim	144
restraints of trade	143
Sherman Act violation	141
Sherman Antitrust Law	138
Single Firm Conduct	143
state insurance regulates	145
unreasonable methods	143

Appeals

appeal - how to file	29,147
appeal - when you can	185
appeal brochure EN-05-10041	185
appeal Form, SSA-561-U2	185
appeal info Chapter 12	41
appeal process	186
appeal rights	147,185
appeal where to file	147
appeal witness at hearing	187
cost to appeal	29,147
decision favorable	191
decision first ALJ	190
decision second ALJ	190
decision unfavorable	190
disagree determination	187
fail to submit form case ends	190
FREE appeals	185
help from local office	170
how offsets are calculated	187
Judge conference held	148
legal representation	147
POMS, code number	147
presenting your case	148
printout of hearing	148
reconsideration form	170
recording of appeal	148
Request Reconsideration	185
Review Council	191
SSA Review form HA-520	190
strategies used by SSA	133

taking appeal to next level	187
video of appeal hearing	187
web: ssa.gov/appeals	185

B

Beneficiaries

church, or a charity	169
family members, spouse	169
married spouse / child	168
permanent choice	19
predetermined beneficiary	163
right to choose beneficiaries	168
survivors	12

Benefits

annuities, time certain	100
average benefit in 2015	22
beneficiary, benefits	19,100
benefits congress $139,200	108
benefit cuts possible	32
benefit determinations	163
benefit disabled reduced	14
benefit promises a lie	31
benefit propaganda	32
benefit, death	168
benefits an earned right	128
benefits denied	128
benefits for women	76,77
benefits inadequate	15
benefits paid by taxpayers	14
benefits under attack	14
born between 1943 - 1954	23
cost, the biggest	87
Dual E info Chapter 7	87
Dual Entitlement offset	9
earnings needed / quarter	12
earnings women/ minorities	30
eligibility failed	106
eligible calendar quarter	21
eligible years, no earnings	28

emergency withdrawals 102
how benefits / calculated 187
how retirees are fleeced 60, 80
how to become eligible 25
how to get largest benefit 21
low ½% Rate of Return 118
low earnings average 173
low earners hurt most 122
men, avg. benefit amount 22,
offset regulation conflicts 107
offset unintended conseq 48
PIA choosing acct 89
PIA married choices 9
Primary Insurance Acct 21,88
private acct. advantages 101
shortages, benefits 124
skimpy SS benefits 99
SS benefits no options 99
SS covered work 129
state no SS credits 177
state pension benefits 114
statements not accurate 27
survivor benefits 14
taxes on benefits 103
taxpayer will never bail out 114
Vanguard Index 500 117
wages needed per quarter 21
wealthy receive largest 104
WEP calculation 605.383 65
WEP or GPO never both 49
WEP, takes up to half 99

Bills

bills now in Congress 154
committee review 160
how bills become law 160
Kevin Brady 159
Richard Neal 159
senate votes on 160

Bonds, Special Issue T-bills

annual rate 117
combined bond returns 117
Congress forces purchases 129
default on paying back 138
government - created 120
inflation effect 119
interest due trust fund 139
investment choices 125
junk bond rating - definition 137
meager returns ½ of 1% 104
negative returns 85
purchasing power loss 135
safe but poor performance 163
t-bill bond rate 2012 117
t-bill special issue SS 112
trustees annual report 118
underperforming bonds 85,13
yields are very, very poor 134

Books

Beyond Outrage 166
Get What's Yours 70
Inequality For All 166
Social Security Works 16
documentary/Robert Reich 166

Boycotts

boycott states with offsets 162
boycott, intimidation 145
protesting using boycotts 162

Brady, Kevin

COLA meager 0.39% 183
Equal Treatment Act 159
H.R. Bill 5697 159
idea of fairness 160
offset, formula more fair 39

C

Calculations

conflicting offset answers	107
earnings less than 35 years	12
earnings reduced	36
life expectancy number	78
lump sum WEP calculation	50
new retirees, 76 mo. extra	58
penalty, how calculated	2
spouse benefits reduced	8
Tier 1 40 % to 90% rate	167
Tier 3 poor never reach	166
using your SS earnings	51
wages earned after 60	13

Civil Servants

bus drivers	17,67
civil servants	26
civil servants / scapegoats	167
civil servants singled out	48
earned the right to collect	130
how you get "equalized"	49
incomes, offsets reduce	50
janitors	67
jobs dangerous / deadly	67
moving to different state	42
older workers caught	167
pensions less than peers	67
pensions received	106
police and fire dept.	17
poverty for some	26
professors	17
public employees	25
receiving a "windfall"	49
retired civil servants	98
retirees vilified	26
singles out / penalizes	128
state, city, local workers	17
teachers served country	65
test for civil service workers	26
thinking of young people	32
treated differently	73
voices not heard	132
word "match" is incorrect	63

Civil War Pensions

first SS pension	109
Social Security begins	109

COLA vs Colorado

average increase 2017	115
bonus one-time check	172
can buy bread or gas	115
COLA announcement	171
COLA forecasting inflation	172
COLA guarantee needed	171
COLA SS can afford raise.	181
COLA vs federal pay raise	183
vs	
Colorado State PERA	114
CO average pension	173
CO contributions / earnings	178
CO financially trained	114
CO guarantees COLA	172
CO investments	114
CO lump sum mandatory	178
CO markhillman.com	114
CO PERA Pension Agency	172
CO promised benefits	114
CO refunds contributions	178
CO taxpayer backed	114
CO uses highest 3-5 years	173
CO variety of investments	114

Commissioner of SS

board 3-man abolished	110
conflict of interest	112
dictatorship	85
figurehead	124
has sole authority	16
lack of empathy	45
legally overturn decisions	16
modified "life expectancy"	54
Nancy Berryhill, new 2017	45
out of touch	124
one-person now controls	110
reports to President	196
reluctant to take action	124
SS spares no expense	132
SS above the law	138
strategic plan not developed	122
unquestioned power	132
Title One - Act of 1932	110

Complaint Letter

competition free/ unfettered	140
complaint action plan	121
complaint letter	195
complaint, how to file	195
modified life POMS 605.364	54
original complaint	185
response time reduced	189
Section 5:15 U.S.C. § 45(a)(1).	142
SS letter mailed 3 days late	189
SSA Pub No. 05-10071	195
treated unfairly	195
web hallex www.ssa.gov	194

Congress

average pension	108
average lifelong pensions	108
$104 Billion Afghanistan	134
$43 million on gas station	135
$66 billion rebuilding	134
$900 billion a year spent	136
bills brought to House	160
brain-numbing old policies	121
catastrophic prediction	122
chasing shadows	167
cheap loans for Congress	118
civil servants abused	98
Colorado 2% yr. increase	115
Colorado generous pension	115
Congress Contact info	196
Congress drains fund dry	133
Congress exempted some	145
Congress granted power	16
Congress never amended	177
Congress Representatives	14,19
delusional thinking	167
demand Congress action	157
discriminate civil servants	129
elephant in the room	44
gave SSA the opportunity	62
help low-income retirees	164
How Dem/ Rep views differ	163
income inequality failed	163
inequality women/minorities	30
influencing the votes	32
Joint Econ. Comm. report	27
low-cost money to spend	132
Medicaid / Social Security	164
nothing was changed	38
offset penalties not fair	75
other gov't programs	97
outdated invest. policies	122
persuaded to repeal	153
piggy bank for Congress	118
plundering the Trust Fund	134
power to write regulations	45
repaying SS Trust Fund	138
Representative contact info	153
Senators, contact info	158
seniors - greedy geezers?	16
siphons away money	134
sits while SS system tanks	122

SS Refinancing Act 1983 25
SSA blessing of Congress 106
unable to see big picture 97
viewpoint of Democrats 163
viewpoint of Republicans 163
welfare more expensive 98
welfare propaganda 139
who's on your side 163
young vote for SS "fix" 32
your pension offsets 51

Consumer Price Index CPI

one CPI does not work 181
senior CPI more accurate 181
Warren, Eliz. Apwu.org 181

Corporations

$17 billion only traceable 134
$21 billion spent 134
avoid paying taxes 134
bonus loophole 181
commercial farms 134
corp $77 billion tax breaks 133
corp 288 with subsidies 135
corp highly profitable 134
corp shelter profits 134
corp top five with subsides 133
corporation, article 136
General Electric / Verizon 133
IBM, Wells Fargo, AT&T 133
millions of dollars missing 134
money impossible to track 137
money missing 134
subsidies build race tracks 134
subsidies for video games 134
subsidies to make movies 134
subsidies to oil companies 134
tax loopholes in tax code 135
tax write-offs 135
web ctj.org/corporate tax 134
web thefiscaltimes.com 135

Costs

$62 billion cost to repeal 136
cost SS spends / appeals 130
cost-benefit analysis 111
costs magically disappear 167
expenses do not disappear 96
legal department 130
prescription costs 96
retirees obstacles / hurdles 167
skimpy 0.39% COLA 183
SS excuses, why no COLA 181

Courts

attorney fees outweigh award 192
attorney twist laws to favor 128
benefit of going to court 191
best web sites 193
brief the three parts 193
brief sample Appendix E 193
cannot complete response 189
check number / days given 191
Civil Court book Amazon 192
Civil Procedures - book 192
confirming fax received 189
confirming fax was sent 188
cost to file in District Court 191
costs to represent yourself 191
courts do not rewrite reg. 195
help Cornell web site best 192
web site Cornell is best 192
what is a "pro se" plaintiff 192

Court - District

attorney free if qualified 192
brief filed using the internet 194
brief filing civil action 191
brief - filing in District Court 192
brief forms/instructions 192
brief how to file civil action 193
brief how to write 192

brief laying out the sections	193
brief write and file yourself	192
brief writing format leeway	192
brief, Guild to Brief Prep.	193
civil court sample web site	193
Civil Rule 4 and Rule 26	193
court not impartial	132
courts intimidated by SSA	132
courts rubber-stamp	134
courts do not amend	11
date SS received your doc	191
day stamped on the receipt	189
deadline is date received	191
deadline miss lose / default	131
deadlines may change	191
deadlines must be met	189
deadlines short time	194
decisions are snail-mailed	188
district court last resort	192
documents may be lost	188
fax "mail box full" message	190
fax call SS for working num.	190
fax confirmation printout	188
fax often fails to be received	188
fax use local SSA office	188
fax, for free, documents	186
fax, using other fax machines	188
Illinois Court decision	139
Illinois Court upheld	116
Illinois Judge John Belz	116
lost your appeal case	194
mail always send registered	189
mail envelopes evidence	189
mail keep registered receipt	189
mailing your letter to court	195
mailing, or hand delivering	186
ninth.court.state.OH	193
notify you by snail-mail	186
one-sided justice	132
representing yourself	186
request for time extension	194

SS lavishly spends legal	130
SS retirees fight alone	27,33
SS stacked deck	131
SS staff answers questions	192
SS support personnel costs	129
SSA attorney average pay	130
SSA fights retirees	130
SSA has unlimited cash	132
taking SSA to district court	192
Tenth Circuit Court case	54
time extension how to file	194
U.S. Court of Appeals	194
verify regulation correct	11
web courts.oregon.gov	193
when it's time to STOP	194
when to stop going to court	194
www.law.cornell.edu/rules	193
www.peoples-law.org/court	193

D

Death Benefits

bankrupting event	98
beneficiary, no one eligible	168
bills and funeral expenses	169
cost house repairs	94
cost lawn / leaf removal	94
cost of hiring others	94
cost public transportation	94
cost replace an appliance	94
cost vehicle insurance	94
cost vehicle maintenance	94
costs to settle the estate	169
death benefit a joke - tiny	103
death benefit should increase	168
diet changes	181
diet, poor nutritional	95
GPO offsets for survivor	89
hardship/ stress on spouse	169
home, must give up	95

income loss	169
income lowers life style	169
life style downsized	98
nursing home	95
SS check should continue	169
SS keeps death benefit	168
transitional benefits	169
transitional death benefits	98

Dual Entitlement

average Dual offset $580	90
DE offset deductions	87
Dual E overview	2
Dual E info Chapter 7	87
Dual E, marriage penalty	31, 88
Dual Entitlement problem	179
example of DE offset	88
if both spouses are alive	88
Jon Forman "The Taxman"	179
need to eliminate / update	179
spouses pay two offsets	90
when Dual E began	87

E

Equalization

civil servants singled out	162
equalization is not working	66
financially "equalized"	161
meant to equalize all	168
media name "entitlements"	14
President Reagan began	14
WEP information Chapter 5	45
WEP offset provision	47

F

FICA

bad idea, raising taxes	122
employer pays equal amt.	101
FICA - 165 million pay tax	19
FICA funds is our money	130
FICA agreement is broken	115
FICA cap, raise higher	123
FICA contributions 2017	21
FICA is pre-paid insurance	12
FICA lifetime total tax paid	118,17
FICA rate 2017 is 7.65%	20
FICA tax is mandatory	163
FICA taxes	180
Heritage Foundation	118
IRA's, 401(k), SEP, ROTH	99
payroll deductions for FICA	27
provide retirement options	98
refunds for spouse	115
refunds of FICA taxes	94,10
returns meager ½%	104
returns Vanguard 10.84%	118
SS a profit of $278,000	171
SS active when pay FICA	115
SSA Contribution Refunds	177
taxes paid while employed	110
Trust Fund keeps all FICA	177
wages subject to FICA	123
wages taxed to $127,200	20
wealthy executives, 401(k)	104
worker dies	106
worker pays $628,912	104
workers paid FICA taxes	73

File and Suspend

book "Get What's Your's"	70
file and go back to work	123
file and suspend loophole	123
financial advisors wrote	123
Pinnacle Advisory Group	123
Senior Freedom / Work Act	123

G

Goal

goal, final	184
law for rich & one for poor	153
small changes work best	153

Government Pension Offset

about GPO	2, 8
independent loses all	71
dependent receives all	92
GPO penalty example	74
GPO average man's offset	77
GPO information Chapter 6	71
GPO needs limit of 50%	180
GPO penalty is two-thirds	71
GPO reg. Appendix E	239
GPO Table	78
GPO women average offset	76
income rents / unearned	73
income, when is it earned	72
income, when it is unearned	73
Life Expect. modification	78
panhandlers	74
pay two offsets, GPO & DE	90
POMS GPO GN2608.100	239
spousal benefit / nothing	6
spouse deceased earnings	51
SS unable to determine	36
surviving spouses' GPO	169
survivors - 9 of 10 lose all	71
unearned income	74
women living in poverty	77
working spouse "equalized"	75

Grandfather Clause

grandfather clause needed	167
low-income means test	168
notification never required	167
offsets began 1983	167
offsets destructive	167
retirees/ lose every dollar	167
welfare, benefits / income	168
workers are robbed	167
workers prior to 2004	167

Groups

joining a group / free	150
joining / supporting groups	157
meetings, speak up	150
open discussions	150
organizations Appendix C	217
ssfairness.com	157
voices of many are barking	150

H

Health

poor diet / declining health	95
bills will stress out spouse	95
emergency room visits	95
medical expenses increase	95
SS and Medicare	183
heating expense	96

I

Income

income decides penalty	29
income severely reduced	95
SS reduced offset penalty	24
unearned income	73

Independent Agency

Environmental Protection	110
Independent Agency	110
serve "at the pleasure"	110
vs	

Regulatory Agency

cost-benefit analysis, no	111
only be removed for cause	110

power to dismiss is limited 110
president cannot control 110
SSA is regulatory agency 110

Insurance - SS

fund pays workers 12
spouse / children covered. 11
wages / job / disabled lost 12
worker protection 11

Investments by SSA

all the eggs in one basket 120
annuities guarantee 99
annuity belongs to company 100
benefits only one SS option 21
bond has 1.37% return rate 117
bond rate appeared decent 118
bonds "special issue" T-bills 84
bonds deteriorated badly 119
bonds low returns past years 118
bonds returned 1/2 of 1% 61
cost to manage Trust Fund 125
if born after 1966 118
Index 500 returned 16% 117
invest to replace lost SS 81
law archaic / discriminatory 121
news sec.gov/news 121
offset fixed at imaginary 6% 61
offset rate fixed forever 60
oversight of market stability 121
retirees lose a lot of money 138
retirees not saving 61
SS violated two basic rules 120
stock market pressure 121
stocks $8.6 trillion a day 121
stocks made 11 times more 117
stocks outperform bonds 120
Trust Fund holding bonds 121
Trustees forced by law 172
Vanguard returned 32% 117
web vanguard.com VFINX 118

J

Judges

apples vs oranges 198
Judge Lyle Douglas Olson 197
Judge Olson 54
judges cannot repeal 11
LE table. not interchangeable 199
lifetime of a lump sum 54
offset ending date 174
offset repeats over & over 175
offset should stop at end of 174
offsets would never end 199
Olson, demanding, strict 197
Olson, Fargo, North Dakota 197
outrageous argument 59
Sangamon County ruling 116
SS benefits restored if 175
SS plays with stacked deck 131
SSA overturned decision 82,19
SSA's accusations 198
tables not interchangeable 199
web ndcourts.gov 197

L

Laws

custom-tailored law for few 65
file / suspend discontinued 124
Judge made "error in law" 83
law requires you participate 103
law twisted to favor the SSA 106
laws apply to state pension 116
repealing this terrible law 167
SS Act Section 201(d) 120
web www.crs.gov RL33028 122
WEP Public Law 98-21 47

Life Expectancy

Actuarial Study	78
average COLA about $5.00	183
chart four LE for same age	78
Email for Steve Mnuchin	183
how long you will live	57
information Appendix E	199
judge said chart not LE	198
LE "modified," / changed	170
LE changed 37 to 12 years	175
LE cut double/triples offset	170
LE cut in half by the SSA	79
LE men / women is same	55
LE modified doubles offset	3
LE POMS 605.364 law	199
LE real Study, No. 120	170
LE same for women / men	170
Life Tables Appendix E	175
Lifetime Actuarial Values	199
lifetime of a lump sum	198
man 65 yr. life expectancy	170
men / women Real LE	78
modification doubles offset	175
modification robs retirees	170
modifications must stop	170
offsets calculated by SSA	77
offsets increase / modify	175
POMS full version	239
SS LE Calculator	199
SSA Actuarial Dept.	198
Steve ask him anything	86
tables do not look same	199
Treasury Sec. Jacob Lew	183
web ssa.gov/oact/NOTES	170
web www.treasury.gov	183
woman 65, how long lives	170
your "real" life expectancy	55

Legal

attorney, do not hire	192
attorney, free assistance	40
brief, the three parts	193
cell phones call records	189
Cert of Serv. Appendix E	194
Certificate of Service copy	193
compromise is not possible	132
date on letter, not envelope	189
divide and conquer	106
juggernaut of SS attorneys	40
justice system is a joke	85
legalized robbery	106
letters - keep everyone	189
losing by missing deadline	189
SS numerous appeals	133
SS overturns decisions	85
SSA never receives doc's	189
SSA twists meaning of laws	79

Library

how to keep up demand	156
how to promote book	155
lack of demand/book is sold	156
local library	155

Lump Sum

beneficiary's lifetime	53
calculating lump sum	176
calculating new lump sum	176
current interest rate not used	176
depletion schedule not used	175
ending date is last month	176
expected life of lump sum	174
fixed 6% rate of return	176
how long lump sum will last	174
interest rate updated / year	177
lifetime of a lump sum	82,19
lifetime vs life expectancy	82
lump sum always invested	176
lump sum balance zero	84,17
lump sum depleted	62,175
lump sum is divided by LE	78
lump sum offset trigger	173

no adjustment/ withdrawals	176
poor health it's best option	18
specific time period	51
SSA eventually takes 200%	177
SSA says never depleted	59
T-bill rate vs lump sum rate	177
unobtainable fixed returns	176
using LE to divide lump sum	55
WEP information Chapter 5	47
why is rate never adjusted?	176

M

Marriage

benefits all or nothing at all	179
claiming SS on partner	178
credits every year married	180
Dual Entitlement, DE offset	4
fail to meet 10-years	179
GPO marriage penalty	31
GPO offset deduction	27
lifestyle differences	179
marriage a must to qualify	178
no credits for your account	179
time for SS to modernize	179
why 10-Yr. marriage rule?	178

Match

capital gains it is!	63,17
dividends are earnings	173
interest earned	173
matching funds are actually	173
offsets stop if no match	173
requires you take match	173
right to refuse the match	174
rule change/matching funds	174
share of the earnings	177
small SS benefit / offsets	173
state "match" trap	173
why refuse the match	173

Migration, The Great

cost shifting not the answer	168
costly migration	166
costs the government more	96
expenses do not disappear	166
expenses also migrate	96,166
food stamps 48 mil receive	68
government agencies/ other	96
homeless seniors increase	166
Medicaid	96
Migration, The Great	96
nothing changes	168
repetitive paperwork	166
retirees apply/ food stamps	96
retirees needs do not stop	166
retiree's shift living costs	97
retiree's turn to welfare	68
seek rental assistance	96
seniors just migrate	168
seniors seek financial help	166
seniors and endless forms	166
SS closes the front door	166
SS seniors use back door	166
SS shortsighted strategy	97
water amount is the same	167
water pouring into glass	167
which agency now pays	168

Minorities

hurt the most.by offsets	29
minorities paid less wages	30
offset exempt never qualify	28

Motherhood Penalty

Al Gore	104
moms often take years off	104
motherhood penalty	179
SS punishes mothers	179
web jay.law.ou.edu	180

N

Notification

ample time never defined	80
delayed for 25-years	81
information Chapter 4	35
notification vague POMS	44
officially "notified" in 2005	80
SSA-1945 "notification"	80
SSPA Public Law #108-203	35

O

Offsets

Al Gore, motherhood penalty	105
ask if offsets have end date	187
computer detects fraud	1
court vs repealing offsets	132
DE affects greatest number	87
DE not either / or exchange	88
DE takes dollar for dollar	88
Defense, Fin., Acct. Ser.	65
Dual Entitlement, DE	51
eliminating the offsets	26
equalization problem	76
example, DE if married	9
failed to pay offsets due	1
few are exempt PL108-375	65
fire and police dept.	65
fixed offset rate needed	167
gov't believes little hardship	66
gov't pension & offsets	26
GPO maximum penalty	74
GPO not limited to 50%	73
grandfather clause needed	32
high paid males favored	33
how GPO offsets calculated	8
how WEP offsets calculated	7
Info Dual Chapter 7	87

information GPO Chapter 6	71
information WEP Chapter 5	47
judge said offsets do end	82
law out-of-sight 21 years	115
law seemed logical once	69
LE modification doubles	78
life expectancy confusion	77
low wages high offsets	167
married spouse - 2 offsets	4
men are only 2% who pay	88
messy offset maze	106
military, no offsets	65
no lump sum adjustment	84
no bill to end the offsets	135
offset fights Dem vs Rep	37
offset mess	107
offset same for everyone	167
offsets affect 6.5 million	76
offsets are complicated	37
offsets begin, Reagan	25
offsets but no SS credits	186
offsets hurts these workers	122
offsets may be tripled	170
offsets not repealed soon	32
offsets repeat over & over	175
offsets will not end	175
old formula one-size-fits-all	33,85
overview of three offsets	2
pay offsets for how long	107
penalty same for all options	50
pension $1, offset takes $3	166
poor pay the largest offsets	27,16
poor, gov't penalizes	122
remaining bal. lump sum	60
repeal - costs for 10 years	98,13
retirees made to feel guilty	161
retirees offsets/ homeless	23
rich some do not pay offsets	99
rich reduced offset penalty	94
scapegoats, civil servants	26
siphons away your pension	51

INDEX 275

spouses could lose all SS 27,10
SS the offset gravy train 43
SS offset appeals are free 40
SS returns millions back to 63
SS says offset never end 175
SSA greedy double-dipper 60
SSA no exceptions 24,29
state sole decision maker 54
Subcommittee Soc. Sec. 36
substan. earnings- fail test 28
triple offsets for young 170
Trust Fund regulations 115
two charts compare LE 55
two offsets if married 90
wealthy pay no offsets 92
web www.NEA.org 44
web www.ssfairness.com 44
WEP brochure No.05-10007 8
WEP information Chapter 5 47
WEP meant to equalize 67
WEP offsets/p to 50% 6
WEP reduction is limited 27
WEP, GPO, DE penalties 24
when lump sum is gone 57
when offsets should stop 84
when your pension ends 175
who has to pay offsets 18
who pays largest offsets 78
women 98% of offset group 76
workers caught off guard 115
you get what you pay for 93

P

Penalties

appealing offset penalties 184
civil service penalties 5
government civil service 18
law is worthless 83
no exemption low income 167

offset penalties 25,27
penalties same for all 29
penalties WEP and GPO 161
penalty int. rate adjusted 84
rich have few/no penalties 76
SS overpayment - bill sent 3
unpaid offset penalties 1
waiver, how to file a 3
WEP no more than 50% 51

Pensions

civil servants/sm. pension 67
collecting two pensions 49
contribute to retire. acct. 20
gov't only have offsets 73
if LE small-offsets larger 78
offsets should then stop 57
participation required 114
pay SS regardless of state 116
private retirement accounts 99
purpose to deny benefit 106
retirees run offset gauntlet 30
SS benefits cut if shortfall 114
SS needs/ increase benefit 50
state pension- guaranteed 114
St. pension triggers offsets 99
state pension - you lose SS 162
time when offsets stop 51
working class pay offsets 73

Petitions

how to start a petition 158
petition Congress to repeal 175
petitions 153
web www change.org 158
www.thepetitionsite.com 158

POMS

Comm. can write laws 16,62
Congress/ Pres. can amend 11
no grandfather clause 24

notification RS 01505.001	35
Dual E POMS RS00615.020	89
POMS contradictory laws	36,10
POMS GPO poorly written	62,79
POMS laws / regulations	30,19
POMS WEP full version	239
Pro Oper. Manual System	115
Pro Operations Manual	2,10
purpose law--withhold SS	30
quagmire of confusing laws	107
regulations, finding codes	2
request President repeal	11
search POMS on internet	11
www.socialsecurity.gov	165
WEP reg. RS605.364	239

Poor - Low Income

adding second pension	166
average wages $29,930	166
corp. subsidy 3x rent assist.	135
crushing offsets	168
disadvantaged poor	20,27
expenses elec./heat bills	96
expenses force diet chg.	95
expense force home sale	95
feast/famine/unemployment	28
increasing retirement age	32
largest offset penalties	99
less earned/higher offsets	166
no offset exemption for poor	32,180
Offset Refinancing Act	26
penalties / poorest of poor	26,16
poor get poorer	166
poor pay highest penalties	166
poor working into poverty	166
punishing the poor retiree	76
rate high 90% for the rich	180
rate low 40% for the poor	180
Reagan poor - poorer	15
retirees swamping welfare	167
retirees with low incomes	168

seasonal workers	28
SS game jump/climb/crawl	167
web obliviousinvestor.com	166
without income exemption	32
women and minorities	29
workers / low-wage jobs	23
working part-time gov't job	166

Presidents

demand SS Comm. resign	112
Pres. Clinton EO #12866	111
Pres. Franklin D. Roosevelt	4
Pres. Reagan-Entitlements	14
president - how to contact	155
president@whitehouse.gov	155
The White House - mail	155

Pres. Reagan, Rep

air traffic controllers fired	14
cut gov't welfare programs	168
cut spousal/disabled benefit	164
disabled, homeless, poverty	164
eliminate heat/food assist.	164
eliminate unemploy ins	164
goal to reduce government	164
government is too big	163
income inequality rose	14
one stupid idea	164
Reagan created POMS	112
Pres. & SSA Commissioner	112
Repub. dislike programs	164
SS Refinancing Act 1983	25
too much welfare spending	163

President Roosevelt, D

began Social Sec. for all	109
death benefits added	109
disabled added	109
spouses / children covered	109
SS expanded by Roosevelt	109
welfare assist. increased	109

President Trump, R

President Trump	141
web finance.yahoo.com	138

Private Retirement Accounts

401(k) plan	20,164
401(k) retirement plan	101
annuity monthly payments	18
beneficiary gets payments	100
Brookings Institution report	164
web www.brookings.edu	164
How Would Invest./Equities	164
choose your investments	102
company pensions gone	23
Hillary Clinton, Vanguard	117
priv. invest. acct. advant.	101
ROTH, IRA or 401(k)	61
San Diego switch to 401(k)	5
Soc. Sec. Protection Act	35
SS acct. avg. worth $2 mil	104
SS plan disadvantages	101
SS withdrawals required	61
SSA keeps all your money	102
St. participation/fragmented	5
state decision irreversible	5
state investment options	99
state lump-sum payout	18
state pension options	50
tax-free ROTH accounts	102

Protests

"How to Protest" web site	150
Facebook/Twitter, YouTube	150
fragmented approach	150
getting the door open	153
grass root protests	149
how to get the ball rolling	149
Illinois protest case filed	116
it takes just one	149
leader to rally others	149
leader, movement needs	149
offsets will continue	62
people, some unable to act	149
protest for repeal of offsets	149
Rosa brought awareness	151
Rosa Parks Story	151
Rosa refused to sit in back	151
Rosa www.biography.com	151
single person	149
start a protest movement	150
stop every man for himself	150
support and guidance	149
take action	152
uniting to demand change	106
where to begin	152
write emails	152

R

Robert Reich

abuse land and cattle	165
big corporations	165
book "Beyond Outrage"	166
book "Inequality for All"	166
crony capitalism	165
documentary award-winning	166
environmental damage	165
factory farms	165
former Secretary of Labor	165
giant food processors	165
harm consumers	165
lobby/campaign contributions	165
monopoly power	165
squeeze the farmers dry	165
stop the huge subsidies	164
sweetheart deals	165
taxpayers fund programs	165
web www.robertreich.org	165
what Robert Reich said	164

Repeal

asking Congress to repeal	153
cost eliminate GPO/WEP	136
email and Twitter	155
email's for Rep Appendix A	154
goal is to repeal	153
how to avoid the long delay	155
how to get Rep's attention	152
letter sample Appendix D	196
letter snail mail 2-3 months	154
letters screened / x-rayed	154
many voices bring attention	154
need all offsets repealed	184
one item at a time	153
petitions can be effective	155
POMS reg. one big mess!	106
retirees offsets are cruel	98
smaller bite size pieces	153
too much numbs receiver	152
web waysandmeans.house	154

Representatives

asking for offset repeal	174
Congress does not see	97
Congress powerful message	150
Congress pressure	149
Congress, protesting to	150
Congress takes notice	150
Congress web / messages	154
Congress Representatives	152
contact www.house.gov	154
contact www.senate.gov	154
contact phone calls	153
contact preferred methods	155
demand action	150
How To Eat an Elephant	152
info Congress Appendix A	201
pay raise 2.1% fed. emp.	183
pay raise 0.39% COLA	180
Reagan reduced benefits	163
SS representatives	107

Retirees

age, you must be to retire	163
blue-collar workers	122
cannot afford to hire help	96
chances of living in poverty	77
Congress false beliefs	66
deceived workers for years	33
diet changes - less healthy	95
equalizing the poor	168
exempt poor from offsets	65
face max. GPO penalty	75
fail substant. earnings test	30
fear SS will go bankrupt	14
file / suspend discontinued	123
file/suspend began filing	123
four qtrs. / calendar year	21
full retirement benefits	163
higher medical expenses	94
household expenses same	94
how or where to appeal	29
increase your SS benefits	22
loans written off as a "loss"	138
low retirement income	167
lump sum if short LE	18
married collecting/ spouse	4
meant to pay benefits	138
media demeaning names	16
name calling-dbl dippers	48
need to change old policies	121
not able to receive 100%	26
penalizes low-income	23
physically demanding jobs	123
PIA - may choose account	21
principal is our money	139
private plan--no offsets	102
propaganda effective	15
propaganda demonizes	32
qualified denied SS	107
retiree cannot pay bills	133
retiree fights the SSA alone	33
retiree's fail to appeal	29

retirees/conflicting answers 36
retirees/food stamps/heat 68
retirees draining fund 32
retirees aware of loophole 124
retirees lose $100 billion yr. 88
retiree no benefits 106
retirees passively accept 92
retirees resort to shoplifting 97
retirees spending over 61
retirees cannot pay bills 23
retires no longer saving 61
reverse mortgages 68
siphon your whole pension 51
Social Security FICA taxes 19
SS is a financial safety net 26
SS major source of income 101
SS no retirement options 163
SS overpayment bills 1
SS withholds benefits 113
SSA fantasy 42
SSA is double dipping 60
state match triggers offsets 63
statistics do not include 67
unable to support yourself 72
unaware and dumbfounded 167
unchallenged DE rule 90
who really loses 137
women at-home caretaker 30
women live in/near poverty 68
worked / rightfully earned 98
workers left to flounder 80
workers left to struggle 98

Rich

FICA cap is $127,200 - 2017 20
FICA tax - no longer pay 20
high 90% rate for wealthy 180
idle rich vs working poor 73
invest. income not counted 73
loopholes & chump change 136
no GPO / non-work spouse 73

Reagan rich became richer 15
sub. earn. large incomes 28
tax write-offs for wealthy 134

S

Schools

bus drivers, secretaries 17
coaches & assistants 17
principals/ directors 17
school lunch workers 67

Seminars

address specific issues 158
advertise seminars 156
articles - local newspaper 157
attendee's emails, phone # 157
blips on your local TV 156
contact info for seminar 156
copy of book for viewing 155
discount coupons available 154
discussion at end 157
flier outlining time/ topics 155
free seminars at work sites 155
info on where to buy book 154
issues to challenge 150
library info desk fliers 155
mail or hand deliver fliers 156
newspapers, invite reporter 156
places home/church/library 150
radio stations, TV stations 156
Rosa Parks/media success 151

Seniors

called old greedy geezers 16
cannot afford to retire 171
CPI of what seniors buy 181
death benefit increase 98
decent standard of living 171
diet and food choices 95

Emergency Benefits Act 181
health largest expense 181
health cut their pills in half 95
help Am./repeal offsets 135
higher Part B premiums 183
jobs seniors hold 171
key source of income 135
Medicare grim news 183
migrate to local food bank 96
migrate to other agencies 166
outpatient care 183
poor reach out for assist. 96
poorest retirees 99
repairs may be postponed 96
retirees ignored / forgotten 58
retirees lose millions 129
retirees run benefit gauntlet 30
seniors more would retire if 171
SS games must crawl 167
unemployment benefits 19
web www.ssa.gov 137
welfare programs 135

Shortages

benefits could be cut 2034 119
need to save Soc. Sec. 25
negative messages 32
poor bond invest. increase 121
prevents revenue it needs 122
raising age not acceptable 122
raise top income / FICA tax 123
resentment/current workers 14
silence is your consent 148
three trillion dollar surplus 85
young / emotional terrorism 32

Social Security

annuities unique option 100
attorney, twist law favor SS 79
average market volume 121

bankruptcy not likely 26
basic facts www.ssa.gov 114
benefit cost 2016 113
benefit earned/promised 116
benefits are skimpy 99
benefits be paid 114
benefits paid state workers 113
benefits will be stopped if 113
cash shortage 119
civil retiree SSA aggressive 99
civil no right to collect SS 32
Clayton Act 141
collect benefits two accts. 9
Commissioner not helping 140
Commissioner has control 163
Commissioner/ disappoint 46
cost-benefit analysis 111
court - SS uses stress 133
court divide-and-conquer 33
credits towards penalty 94
current/past pay records 1
death - transitional benefits 125
death benefits to continue 98
deductions taken forever 175
default on the $3 trillion 137
delaying retirement 22
demonizing gov't retirees 32
die before collecting 178
disability, death, retirement 127
Dual E punishes married 93
earned protection 127
eligibility - 40 qtrs. needed 104
eligible - if you are not 115
eligible earnings 35 yrs. 104
Eligible - $1300 per qtr 21
English felt gov't duty o 109
English felt responsible 109
English Poor Law of 1601 109
entitlements 129
equalizing using offsets 50
Exec Ord. not apply to SS 111

exempt pres. control/EO	111	POMS find code numbers	10
expenses surviving spouse	94	Pres. Reagan's Refin. Act	10
expensive teams attorneys	130	Pres. Roosevelt SS	109
fail to meet 40 quarters	177	private accts.no 40 qtrs.	102
FICA Taxes pay benefits	19	propaganda / workers	32
fiduciary, responsibility is	128	purpose of insurance	127
file/suspend allowed	123	replace income lost	127
file/suspend stopped	124	restoring full SS benefits	176
file/suspend www.aarp.org	124	retirees 43 million 2016	113
file-and-suspend strategy	69	retirees divide/ conquer	150
fixing by increasing FICA	32	retirees SS/Medicare s	12
food reduced or eliminated	95	rich reduce offsets	28
GPO POMS GN 02608.100	71	right to collect on both	91
GPO how offset is calculated	71	rules are over 80-years old	120
Heritage Found. Ctr. Data	118	scapegoats/Refinance Act	26
history SSA www.ssa.gov	109	shortage of funds	25
how SS determines LE	170	shortages Denver Post	119
how to get largest benefit	89	side-step antitrust	145
if seniors had larger benefit	171	smart invest. plan in 1935	119
income high 90% calculate	36	Soc. Sec. - no guarantees	98
income low 40% calculate	36	Soc. Sec. not bankrupt	26
information on WEP Chp. 5	47	Soc.Sec. disadvantages	102
is SS denies your claim	144	Soc.Sec. independent reg.	110
life expect/ alternative facts	56	social insurance concept	127
life expectancy "modified"	53	Social Security Act of 1935	11
loans only to U.S. gov't	112	Social Security history	106
low operating costs	113	spouse may lose all	27
low overhead - who cares?	125	SS "modified" life table	175
lump sum never depleted	175	SS 50% increase	171
media impression welfare	14	SS act above the law	138
migrate /short of money	96	SS based on social insur.	109
misleading statements	7	SS benefit statements	62
notification failed to warn	27	SS benefits inadequate	171
OASDI	127	SS benefits stop if you are	1
offset/do not reduce short.	123	SS Board 3-member team	110
offsets none if not Soc.Sec.	92	SS clerks make errors	44
offsets start Congress	25	SS cuts your LE in half	58
old formulas	85	SS decides benefit amt.	163
original Social Security Act	4	SS deliberately modifies	80
paying benefit claims	128	taxpayers never pay	113
penalizes spouses	8	SS does not offer options	29

SS excuses	128
SS fiduciary responsibility	122
SS has 62,000 employees	113
SS has a vise-grip on	164
SS highly inflates offset	175
SS calculated using 35 yrs.	12
SS is not welfare assist.	109
SS is too stingy	171
SS keeps all contributions	163
SS likes offset status quo	43
SS maximum benefit is	165
SS no COLA guarantee	115
SS no earnings credits	178
SS not being efficient	132
SS NOT a free handout	30
SS NOT a freebie	106
SS NOT based on need	30
SS not held to laws of land	116
SS NOT welfare	30,06
SS office is in Baltimore	113
SS poor returns on bonds	117
SS greedy double-dipper	60
SS salaries	131
SS self-serving regulations	168
SS should invest / equities	120
SS refund FICA taxes	128
SS takes state pension	177
SS threatens retirees	124
SS Treasury bonds	117
SS Trust Fund	61
SS Trust Fund An. Report	117
SS Trust purchases 6/2013	117
SS, gives nothing back	178
SSA Chief Actuary	86
SSA LE modification	79
SSA guts retiree's pension	177
SSA is greedy	170
SSA Judge Olson decision	82
SSA judges, paralegals	131
SSA juggernaut	131
SSA lawyer salary, in 2017	131
SSA legal support staff	160
SSA receives big "windfall"	58
SSA waited until 2004	43
SSA's responsibility to pay	108
statements wrong / far less	27
states switch to Soc.Sec.	5
Steve Goss, Chief Actuary	86
stock market investments	120
substantial earnings	28
surplus $3 trillion dollars	26
taxpayers never pay	113
T-bill rate measly 1.37%	117
Trust Fund is "going broke"	26
Trust Fund - fake news	84,119
Trustees agreement S	115
twitter.com / Social Sec.	86
using 35 years is overkill	173
wages until 60 indexed	13
WEP brochure No.05-10007	8
who's paying SS salaries	133
withholding benefits	97
www.ssa.gov/policy/docs	164
yearly surplus - billions	113
young never receive SS	177
your SS determination	173

Spouses

a few collect 100% of both	66
annuity original investment	100
beneficiary designated	66
collecting on spouse	9,89
death survivor's health	95
divorced or widowed	87
file / suspend discontinued	123
file / suspend what it did	123
GPO may receive nothing	179
history no offsets 1983	91
household income cut half	98
independent work/spouse	92
married eligible in 10 years	87
married eligible immediate	102

married GPO is unlimited	27
married may lose all SS	103
PIA primary ins. acct.	21
spousal pension	179
spouse alive eligible 50%	88
spouse dead eligible 100%	10
spouse entitled to both	180
spouse never worked	92,17
spouse never worked	65,74
surviving spouse pays all	94
survivor benefits	8
two SS benefit accounts	89
unpaid work	178
what is earned income?	72
women 90/100 nothing	71
work/spouse discriminate	76
working spouse nothing x	179

States

agency / no time certain	52
agency does not reveal	174
agency contacts Appendix B	209
beneficiary state options	18
complain direct to agency	196
Dual E covers all 50 states	87
English welfare of citizens	109
highest three-year average	66
Illinois constitu. guarantee	139
Illinois requires state to pay	116
incorrect word "match"	173
info offsets vague/skimpy	174
information state agencies	209
investments avg. 8% yr.	118
match triggers penalty	63
pension forces members	174
petition direct to agency	174
private pension plan	18
San Diego switch to 401(k)	5
short time worker subsidize	67
SS allows only the agency	53
state agency is easier to fix	173

st. agency refuse end date	54
state invest. successful	114
state one in five will qualify	66
st. pensions have options	18
state wants to hire/retain	174
state's private pension plan	107
states / generous pensions	106
states establish pension	5
States with offsets	4
taxpayers back pensions	114
the "Matching" Funds trap	63
typical gov't employee	67
WEP and state pensions	8
workers pay agency salaries	64

Substantial Earnings

civil ser. qualifying hurdle	26
cost 5% each yr less 30	166
fail sub test due low wages	27
favors highly paid workers	27
low 40% low wage worker	164
high 90% for rich worker	164
high paid do not pay	28
how much per year	26
huge drop in percentage	165
less n 20 yr. substan. earn	165
less than 30 yr. substantial	165
over 30 years, pay nothing	26,16
minorities/women pay most	164
outdated offset formula	28
part-time/ seasonal work	164
penalizes most women	164
penalty based on test	172
poor unable to pass test	166
reduce amt. of sub wages	30
reduce to 3 yr avg. earn	180
thirty-five yrs./ is excessive	173
Substantial is regressive	180
rich very few have offsets	172
SS web site: www.ssa.gov	26
Sub Earn #05-10045	167

Sub. corp get $364 billion	133
substantial earnings test	173
Tier 1 level, for the rich	180
typical mom has 27 years	105
upside-down, regressive	27
wealthy easily past test	180
women unlikely to qualify	77
years from 20 to 29	165

T

Taxes / Taxpayers

FICA non-refundable	21
subsidy for wealthy	135
taxable FICA wages 2017	101
taxpayers never pay SS	137

Teachers

largest group /pensions	17
teacher shortages	161
TRTA members	160
vacancies difficult to fill	161

Treasury Bonds

amend investment policies	120
bond returns turn negative	119
low interest bonds lose	119
not a diverse portfolio	120
purchases $253 million	117
special issue T-bills	61
Trustees Annual Report	117

Trust Fund

Annual. Trustees Report	183
below market interest rates	129
benefits fully paid till 2034	26
Fund exhausted in 2034	122
bond investment policy	121
bond purchases report	118
bonds negative return	120
Buffet, Bonds 'terrible'	126

cash outflows from Fund	123
Congress force bond pur.	112
Congress robs Trust Fund	122
financial manager needed	114
financially inept	85
foreign rebuilding projects	134
Fund report out in July	117
Fund took in 897 billion	113
funds squandered	129
government exploits fund	134
junk bonds / a definition	137
laws written decades ago	122
loans difficult to repay	137
lousy returns on bonds	106
Mike Rosen, Denver Post	119
need to update policies	126
only "cost" is interest due	139
out-flows from the Fund	97
Pres. proposed default	138
propaganda of shortages	32
public's fear of shortages	25
responsible to invest	129
retirees need better returns	125
retirees short-changed	119
revenues exceed benefits	112
short term, less one-year	120
shortage in the Trust Fund	121
should stop buying when	129
skimpy 1.37% return	61,17
special issue T-bills	171
SS returns unpaid benefits	44
SS Trustees report	26
stock market invest 5%	121
surplus nearly three trillion	112
surplus ssa.gov/policy	112
surpluses every year	112
treasure chest to be looted	134
Trust Fund losing money	85
Trustee violate rules	120
Trustees Annual Report	85,117
Vanguard Index 500 Fund	117

retirementsecurity.org	136
usgovernmentrevenue.com	113
web www.ssa.gov/history	109

U

Unfairness

inequities in substan. test	30
penalizes low-paid workers	36
reduce competition	142
SSA is not fair to retirees	60
SSA solved unfairness	28
Unfair Competition	142
unfavorable decisions	132
unfavorable determination	147

V

Vanguard Funds

Hillary Clinton	117
Warren Buffet	126
yardstick for comparison	117

W

Warren, Elizabeth, Dem MA

one-time payment of $581	181
Warren Bill # S2251	181
Warren, Eliz., Dem MA	181
without adding a penny	181

Wealthy

divert to private retire. acct.	104
inheritances	73
invest in stock market	104
max of $2,687 month 2017	104
mortgage int. tax deduction	138
multi-million dollars homes	138
real estate investments	73
tax gifts wealthy taxpayers	135

WEB Sites

POMS versions ssa.gov	11
www.ssa.gov/oact/cola	20
ssa.gov/planners/retire	29
nasi.org/learn/soc.security	20

WEP

average SS benefit -wage	165
average WEP offset	68
exploitation of retirees	59
four life expectancies S	78
Gen. Acct. WEP study	36
how SS benefits/ penalized	200
how SS doubles offset amt.	51
how your LE is cut in half	57
hurts part-time workers	67
many do not have pension	67
no match/offsets disappear	63
offset amount is identical	50
offsets appeals constantly	132
POMS 605.364 Appendix E	239
POMS 605.364, Section C	51
purpose of WEP/o equalize	7
recomput.no one qualifies	199
restoring your SS benefits	199
retirees are overpaying	58
retirees need fair formula	39
special treatment: for a few	65
SS Amendments of 1983	47
SS guarantee, WEP limited	31
SS removes "windfall"	7
ssa.gov/pubs/EN-05-10045	164
St. .leaves to exploitation	52
state only can prorate amt.	53
state pension options	50
the real "double-dipper	60
Varied vs Fixed Rate	164
WEP 5% increases	166
WEP formula upside down	164
WEP full reg. Appendix E	239

WEP is mathematic illusion	51
WEP overview	2
WEP up to 50% of your SS	27
WEP's flawed formula	38
when WEP ends	199
when your offsets can stop	57
Windfall logic is illogical	48
worker high paid - rate 90%	165
worker low wage- rate 40%	165

Wicks, Jeanette

buy signed book direct or	24
contact for discounts	184
ssoffsets@yahoo.com	24

Women

affected by GPO 81%	76
average substan. earnings	172
caregiving of elderly	28,17
disparity wages	30
Dual E is harsh to women	90
fail substantial test	28
family caretaker	105
female avg. benefit $1,182	22
few qualify for exemption	77
few women file appeals	145
gov't allows pay gap	180
GPO and surviving spouse	71
index earnings higher ratio	180
instead of 35 years/ lower it	180
issues affecting women	180
lose 34% of their benefits	90
losers 98% n	76
majority who lose all	137
married less than 10 years	106
married 10 or more years	87
married FICA refund	179
min./women hurt most	29
moms stay at home	28,172
most have less than 30 yrs.	172
no additional SS/working	104

paid 66% mid-skill work	77
paid 80% of men	77,180
pay web- iwpr.org//2017	77
poverty 80% higher	77
punished in retirement	68
seldom promoted	77
should reward	180
single one-person house	94
Soc. Security eligibility	21
SSA keeps all FICA taxes	179
SSA treats women unfairly	180
ssa.gov/news/press	23
survivors fear bankruptcy	77
wages even when indexed	173
Who qualifies dependent?	73
why same LE for all	55
women are 98% of total	88
women are vulnerable	23
women fail substan. test	172
women get short-changed	178
women yrs. off careers	172
Women/men receive half	180
work gives nothing extra	180

Workers

administrators	17
ample time/alter retirement	42
book employee's lounge	154
carpenters	28
credits one pension system	48
current workers resentment	15
deny benefits civil servants	25
equipment operators	28
feast to famine	28
GPO applies to workers	73
health issues	28
high paid no FICA taxes	103
idiots work	93
insurance protection SS	11
janitors	166
job entangles you in offsets	81

job links you forever offsets	81		victimized working spouse	93
jobs for younger worker	171		vilified as "greedy takers"	26
jobs physically demanding	42		voter propaganda	32
lack of info - blindsided	62		wages for total lifetime	28
lack of work	28		wages to qualify as quarter	12
low income substan.earn	28		water, sewer, street dept.	17
Michael Kitces	123		WEP regulations	31
moving to new state	43		white-collar workers	123
need to know basis	41		who is penalized	107
non-working spouse	75		women/minorities are hurt	29
oil field workers,	28		work in trades	28
older worker	42		work is for Idiots	93
painters	28		worker could not collect	66
physically wears out body	122		worker dies	106
police and fire department	17		workers earn $29,930	166
police, fire, teachers	154		workers over 60 years old	122
poor pay largest penalties	99		working past full retirement	123
prevent you collecting SS	107		working spouse gets less	75
propaganda fuels jealousy	32		working spouses victimized	93
punishing working women	85			
retires lowest SS benefits	27			
school nurses	17			
seminar at work site	154			
seminar contacts	154			
short-term careers	67			
split careers	69			
sporadic workers, farmers	28			
spouse collects everything	65			
spouse not collect 100%	66			
spouse exempt RS 605.362	65			
SS inefficient sinkhole	139			
SS punishes these women	85			
state match cannot refuse	63			
state, city park employees	17			
substantial earnings test	28			
teachers	17			
temporary, incomes	28			
those who do not work	75			
unable to continue working	122			
unemployed, disabled	12			
union unhappy members	158			

About the Author

Jeanette grew up in Greenfield, Massachusetts and moved to Colorado in 1974. She received her MBA-Finance degree from the University of Denver and is a SEC Registered Investment Advisor.

She worked, for a short time, in the Colorado public school system where she was automatically enrolled in the CO private pension plan – PERA. It was this position that activated her SS offsets.

Now retired, Jeanette learned firsthand about SS offset penalties. Like many others, she was angered by the lack of information which would have prevented her from accepting a public service position in any state with a private pension plan.

She decided to write this book to inform other civil servants about the huge offset penalties they may face if they <u>split their careers</u> between a government job and a SS covered position.

Where to BUY this BOOK

Order directly from your
local book store
or
from Jeanette Wicks
by contacting
ssoffsets@yahoo.com

Also available at:

Amazon   *Barnes & Noble*   *Ebay.*

Many libraries also carry this book

An Ebook or Epub digital book

available in 2018/19

Amazon's Kindle -- Apple IBook
Baker & Taylor – Barnes & Noble
Ingram Spark EPub -- Sony Reader -- Kobo

Quantity discounts are available
with a purchase
of 4 books or more.

Contact: *Jeanette* at: ssoffsets@yahoo.com

CPSIA information can be obtained
at www.ICGtesting.com
Printed in the USA
LVOW03s0021040418
572237LV00001B/115/P